CROSSING the WALL

CROSSING the WALL

a life on both sides

Hui Zhi Song

www.encompasseditions.com

ISBN 978-0-9865203-2-7

Published by EnCompass Editions
Kingston, Ontario, Canada

Cataloguing in Publication Program (CIP) information
available from
Library and Archives Canada
at
www.collectionscanada.gc.ca

COVER: The Chinese characters may be translated as *perseverance*. BACK COVER: The colour photograph shows Hui Zhi Song in rehearsal in Vienna with the Etobicoke Symphony.

interior design by Jean Shepherd (jean.shepherd@videotron.ca)

For my father

Note

In telling this story, I have used my sisters' real names and the real names of my twin nephews, Chen-Hai and Chen-Yong. I have also called Mendel Green, Rochelle Green, Stephen Green and Peter and Carolyn Martin by their real names and of course have used the real names of Chinese public figures. I have substituted pseudonyms for the personal names of others—good and bad—out of respect for their privacy.

BOOK I

Prologue: Chimes at Midnight

My outburst of anger had cured my depression. The rejection by McMaster University was not the end. It occurred to me that I'd been crying much of my life and now I stopped crying. How could I best use the money I'd so painfully saved for my education?

It was 1991. The Canadian economy had gone into recession and the housing market had gone with it. Now was my chance. I called a real estate agent and she led me to a little townhouse on Summerhill Gardens, a five-minute walk from the subway.

The place was messy and run-down but structurally sound, surrounded by old trees, with a big yard that backed onto a wooded ravine—almost a wilderness. I could hardly believe that I could possess something so wonderfully situated. Within a week, I owned it.

I found two Chinese men who had no company or vehicle but did have renovation experience. I offered them a hundred dollars a day each—plus lunch—provided they could finish within two weeks. They agreed and the three of us worked side by side. Rose Wong provided the lunches: sometimes she delivered them herself, sometimes her chauffeur delivered them. We knocked down walls and installed lights in the ceilings and fitted mouldings to hide wires. We sanded and painted the wood floors throughout and built a deck so I could sit outside in good weather.

When we were done I had the shell of my new home but no furnishings. I'd carefully hoarded some money for the next step. At an auction I had bought a mahogany dining table and six chairs before my eye fell on the grandfather clock. It towered above me, a golden musical note set in the middle of its face, and chimed sweetly every fifteen minutes. I fell in love, my heart pounding in my chest, and outbid the room. I went on to buy a Louis love seat and a marble coffee table and then, in a final, mad flourish, a German piano. With that, my budget was exhausted. No, there was just enough for a pair of towels and a pair of winter boots, my first new clothing in seven years. I stood in my own living room in my own house and rubbed the opulent plush of my own towels on my face and neck and wept. My bedroom and other furniture were to be mere chipboard. I couldn't care less.

I had come to understand how wonderful a season autumn is in Toronto: the days sunny, the skies blue, the leaves already starting to change to orange and red. In September of that year, 1992, I had a housewarming party. Rose Wang came of course, and dear Rochelle Green and my professor friends, Terry and her husband, George, and Peter Martin and his wife, Carolyn. Then more and more arrived, all bearing gifts of crystal and china and dishes. I made them a Chinese dinner and we sat at my very own dining room table. The little townhouse was filled with the sound of eating, drinking, talk and laughter.

Around eleven that night, after the last couple had left, I put the dishes in the dishwasher and sat down with a cup of green tea on the Louis love seat. The grandfather clock chimed every fifteen minutes but the world seemed otherwise quite still. My mind turned first to those who had just left that evening and then to those who had stepped out of nowhere to help me in this new land, especially for Green family. I thought of Mendel and Rochelle and Peter and Grandma and all the others who had made the gift of a new life.

Sometime past midnight even the chime seemed to fade. My thoughts deepened and turned to that other house, those many years before, and the mother who still haunted my dreams. And Ling and Li and Guo and Min and little Ping. I thought of Father. Father, how I called you and called but you couldn't answer. I remembered Wu Wu, who played the violin behind the wall. And Teacher Zhou, who hanged herself. And Fa Ling, incorrigible boy. And Grandmother with the tiny, broken feet. And Zhang Wei, who seemed to love me but faded into Thailand. And Lao Ho, who didn't know me and had so little reason to be kind. And hunched up Aunty Lui, my sister's husband's aunt really, who would have let me die for all she cared. And Mother—always Mother—and Chairman Mao, the two strangely linked in my thoughts. The night was flooded with the bitterness and wrongs.

Towards daylight I heard the chimes again. I remembered then how much I'd loved all those people, even those whose hearts had been twisted by experience.

I stood up. I felt feverish and my body ached. I looked out the window at the ravine, still dark but with the sky now brightening above it. How light my heart is, I thought, how unburdened. I went to my new bathroom to take a shower and dress for the day.

1 Dao Chun Long Street

1951-1964

May is the month of rose blossoms in Shanghai, the month of hope and renewal. On the third of May, 1951, at about seven in the evening, a doctor and nurse delivered a baby in the master bedroom of a private house on Dao Chun Long Street. The newborn let out a series of lusty wails and the doctor showed the newborn to the mother.

"Congratulations, madam, you've delivered a healthy baby girl!"

"Another girl?" The mother's face fell. She gave no indication of wanting to hold the child. She gestured to the wet nurse to take it away.

I was that child.

For many years, we were to know nothing about Father's early life. We did, however, know that Mother was born and grew up in Ningbo, in Zhejiang province, one of two children in a middle-class family. She went to high school in her native city but at some point she moved to Shanghai on the other side of the vast Hangzhou Bay, where she began work in the Post Office. At some point she met the man who was to be my father, Song Lian Rei. She was twenty-two and he was twenty-five. We never knew how they met or for how long they courted. They were married in 1941 in Shanghai.

My parents on their wedding day. Shanghai. 1941

I remember my father as a man immersed in his business affairs, so that the family into which I was born hardly saw him. Five daughters and one son had proceeded me, enough apparently that my mother had allowed a friend who couldn't have a baby herself to adopt one of my sisters. The rest of us lived in a three-storey private house in an enclosed community and my parents owned another larger house on the west side of Shanghai. Unlike most of the inhabitants of that enormous city, we enjoyed coal heating, indoor toilets, a bathtub, hot water, three maids, a car and a chauffeur. Three weeks after my birth, my parents named me Song Hui Zhi. Song was our family name. "Zhi" means "stop." Two years later, my mother delivered another girl, whom she named Song Hui

Ping, "Ping" meaning "big quantity, low quality."

My wet nurse had enough milk for me, a chubby baby with big dark eyes, and grownups liked to pinch and squeeze me. My youngest sister was less fortunate. Her wet nurse didn't produce enough milk, she having delivered her own baby some time earlier. Still, she needed the job, so she let my sister suck at her nearly empty breast for five months. Ping's lungs failed to develop properly and she almost died.

After my first year of breastfeeding, I had my own babysitter to look after me and sleep with me, but I have no memory of being hugged by my mother or of her even once holding my hand. I could never quite understand why she was so cold, so unfair, and so strict towards me. Sometimes my brother, who was three years older than me, hit me or pushed me to the ground. If I cried, it was always I who was punished.

I was a pretty little girl but not as home-smart as Ping, who would try to please our mother and brother. Sadly, her strategy failed to meet with much success. I remember playing with her when I was four. My brother grabbed our toy and ran away. We both began to cry and Mother, when she saw this, locked us in a small washroom for hours. Eventually a maid came to the door. "Your mother has a message," she announced. "She says that if you admit the problem was your fault and say you're sorry, she will let you out for lunch." My sister quickly admitted her fault and was allowed out for lunch. I chose to give up the food but keep the truth. As a consequence of such decisions was branded as a stupid and stubborn child.

I often had fevers and my babysitter was eventually charged with taking me to the hospital to have my tonsils removed. When I opened my eyes after the operation, I saw my parents standing beside my bed. They looked big and far away.

Chapter One

"Your mother brought ice cream for you," my babysitter said. She used a spoon to feed it to me and as she did and I saw I was receiving my parents' attention, tears of gratitude coursed down my cheeks. There would be many such tears throughout my life.

When I was five, my father enrolled me in the best kindergarten in Shanghai. The school had good facilities and the best teachers and required students to pass an enrolment test based on aptitude. I was taught singing, dancing, art, math and poetry. I was a fast learner and I enjoyed helping other children. I was popular with most of the teachers and students. I was named the best student in my class for both of years I was there.

One afternoon after our nap, the teachers gathered all ten classes (each class had twenty students) in the square. A man came into the middle of the circle leading a horse, its brown mane shining in the sunlight. We were excited to see this beautiful animal because in a big city it was rare to see such animals outside of a zoo.

"Now," Teacher Lee said, "I will choose one of you to taste the horse's fresh milk and describe its taste to us." All of the hundred pairs of excited little eyes were fixed on her mouth, waited anxiously to see whose name would be called. Suddenly, I heard my name called out. My heart beat faster and I had to suppress an impulse to run in small circles and flap my hands up and down. Instead I walked slowly up to the horse in the middle of the circle. The man with the horse milked it into a glass and handed it the glass to me—the freshest milk I had ever tasted. For the first time in my life I made a speech—and in front of more than two hundred people. all around me were friendly faces and warm laughter.

These two years of kindergarten were the happiest of my

childhood. When they were done, I would of course be enrolled in the best elementary school in the city. That did not happen. Instead, I found myself one morning in a miserable building without tables or chairs. The students had apparently to bring their own. The teachers were housewives who had received only two months of training. Since the space was inadequate, we only attended half days. I was seven and couldn't understand why my circumstances had changed. "It's your father's fault," Mother explained. "Because he's a capitalist."

"If I were not a wealthy capitalist, you wouldn't have married me," Father would answer.

At that time, I knew nothing of my father's background. That would only emerge during the terrible events that lay ahead. For now, to the extent that I understood anything of his work, I understood him to be a successful businessman. He owned a company that made machinery. He owned a bookstore in Shanghai. He was the director of the biggest publishing company in China. Before the Communist Party took control in 1949, most of his friends had taken their money and their families and moved to Hong Kong, but Father had been approached by underground Communist Party members even before the civil war ended and these people convinced him to stay. Anyway, he knew that it was his duty to remain in China because the country needed his talent and knowledge.

After Chairman Mao Zedong proclaimed the People's Republic of China in Tiananmen Square on October 1, 1949, my father and ten friends went to Beijing at Prime Minister Zhou Enlai's invitation. They were held up as examples of successful but patriotic "Red Capitalists." This honour compelled my father to donate the larger of his two houses to Shanghai's city government. Then he moved our family into a smaller house, which had previously been used only for storage. This was the house in which I was born and would spend the next thirty-four years.

Soon the Communist Party began to meddle in the operations of my father's machinery company. In the beginning, he was still kept on as president, with the Communist Party as his manager. After a few years, his position was downgraded, and the Party took full control of the company. My father became a manager whose salary was determined by his political bosses. Soon afterward, the government decided to ban private business. They "compensated" business owners by assessing the value of the business and awarding a "fair" payment without any discussion or negotiation with the owners. They then distributed that payment quarterly over several years. My father soon stopped taking the payments and felt certain that his generosity would demonstrate his support for the government and the country.

In 1956, the Party encouraged my father's former workers to criticize him. He was branded a thief and a leech who had stolen money from his workers and "sucked their blood." He was stripped of his management position. In the spring of 1957, for the betterment of the cause, the Party launched the One Hundred Flowers Campaign and urged intellectuals to criticize officials all the way to the top level. Mao encouraged people to say whatever they wanted to say and to say it to the full. "Mao's intention are to encourage liberalization so that the Communist Party can build a stronger country," said my father. He was happy to offer suggestions.

But only a few insiders knew Mao's real intention: to smoke out the "snakes" that he feared would seek to undermine his march toward a Communist utopia. The result was that anyone deemed an intellectual was labelled a "capitalist" or a "rightist." My father was declared a "fringe rightist." Mao announced that capitalists were on a rampage, attacking China's socialist system. My father was demoted to garbage man and was soon sweeping the floors of the company that he had once owned.

In 1958, Mao started to divide the people along class lines: the capitalist class and the labouring class. By now I understood why I was allowed to attend only the worst school: my father's punishment also applied to his daughter. I tried nonetheless to be a good student and was still appointed class chairman.

That same year, Mao launched the "Great Leap Forward." He declared that China could overtake the steel production of Britain, the original industrial nation, within fifteen years. For the first year, he ordered the nation to double its steel output. In my neighbourhood, uplifting music blared constantly from loudspeakers. Posters declared "Long live the Great Leap Forward!" and "Everybody makes steel!" Although I was only seven and couldn't really understand Mao's order, I found as much steel as I could and brought it to school. I found scrap iron in construction areas far from home or inside garbage cans. It was dirty work, but I was happy to do it, especially since I was a leader in my class.

One Sunday afternoon, the head of our community organization, Comrade Shi, came to our home with three large men. They removed our two steel doors and steel window bars. Comrade Shi said, "Our country needs steel. Your comfort and safety is less important than Chairman Mao's order, isn't it?"

"Yes, of course, Comrade Shi," my father responded. He smiled stiffly. By the time the men left, they had even taken the iron stand I used for washing my long hair.

At seven years old, I wasn't aware that my father had been

branded a fringe rightist and I couldn't understand why he would let people take our doors without any discussion. I did notice that the community leaders from the Party were more powerful than my parents.

In 1959, Father was sent to a labour camp in the north to do hard labour in the fields. While at the camp he received the news that he had stomach cancer. The government allowed him to return home to Shanghai. He went to a hospital, and the doctors there wanted him to stay, but when the hospital management found out he was a member of the "capitalist class," he was refused further treatment.

During the months he was ill at home, all of my siblings attended school full-time, and Mother worked full-time at the post office. I was the only child to attend school for a half day and stay at home the other half. It allowed me to grow closer to my father. He would hold my hand and walk with me to the Yu-Yuan Garden to try different kinds of dim sum. He read to me and once took me to the theatre to watch a 3D movie.

During those months he tried to communicate to me his philosophy of life. "Be a good person and help others without hope for personal gain," he told me. "Intelligent people find a way to bring opposing sides to a mutually beneficial solution." "A greedy person takes for himself and doesn't mind hurting others." "Stupid people do things to hurt others but hurt themselves at the same time." He told me that no important decision should be made before I had thought three times about the consequences, then envisioned the best and worst possible outcomes. "If you can handle the worst, Hui-Zhi, then you should go ahead with the decision." It was a precious time.

After less than a year Father was taken to the hospital for

an operation, but the cancer had spread too far. The surgeons just sewed him back up and told us it was too late. On the second of June, 1961, a month after my tenth birthday, the sound of weeping woke me. Ping and I shared the same bedroom with our maid, each of us with her own bed. The weeping grew louder and I realized it was coming from my parents' room. It frightened me and I began to shake. I covered my head with a blanket. Something was terribly wrong.

My father lay on his funeral bed, his body skin and bones, his hair and beard long and dishevelled. He had been forty-five. I didn't fully understand what death meant, but I understood that he was gone to some place of sleep and would never again return home. As the funeral car left to take his body for cremation, I ran after it in the street. "Daddy!" I cried. "Don't go! I need you! Please don't take my father away! Please!"

At that time in China, we didn't have electric stoves, ovens, washing machines, refrigerators or vacuum cleaners. All housework had to be done by hand. We'd once had a chauffeur and three maids to look after nine peoples' needs. From 1949 to 1961, the number of domestics my father was able to hire dropped from four to one. After he passed away, we could no longer afford to pay our last maid and she too left.

These years—1959 to 1962—were years of famine. All Chinese citizens with the exception of the ruling class went hungry. All food had to be purchased using ration tickets provided by the government. In Shanghai, the monthly food ration for each adult male was thirty pounds of rice, seven ounces of cooking oil, and eight ounces of meat. Female adults got less, and children only received half of an adult male's allotment. Even with money and ration tickets, finding food was difficult. We were lucky in that we received help from my father's friends who had moved to Hong Kong. They shipped food to us from time to time until my father passed away. The rice allowed on one monthly ration ticket would last ten days, and the only way to stretch the ration to the end of the month was to make conge, a rice porridge. The ratio of water to rice was five to one. The market sold no food except bo-bo cai, a vegetable similar to cabbage but with an unpleasant taste. I became lethargic and my face became swollen as a consequence of malnutrition. We heard that in poor villages, hundreds of thousands of peasants had starved to death during the three-year famine. We heard that some were eating soil.

In 1962, Mao announced that the famine's causes were seventy per cent natural disasters and thirty per cent human error. Vice Chairman Liu Shaoqi disagreed with Mao and estimated the reverse. He reasoned that peasants were agricultural workers and knew nothing about steel, but they had been forced to spend their time trying to find and produce steel instead of the food they needed to survive. To make things worse, during the Great Leap Forward, village leaders had tried to please Mao by exaggerating accounts of the amount of food they had harvested, but, mindful of the lessons of 1957's "anti-rightist" movement, no one had the nerve to tell him the truth. More natural disasters struck. The government finally acknowledged a widespread food shortage.

I still had a free half day and Mother put me in charge of the maid's work, including going to the market. After three years of famine, the food supply had finally started to improve, but it remained extremely limited. I would get up between four and five in the morning and line up before the market opened at six. When it did open, no one followed an orderly queue, but everyone rushed in and pushed one other to get to the front. I was squeezed until I could barely breathe.

Sometimes I got a little food and sometimes I returned home empty-handed and full of guilt.

After the nerve-wracking experience of the market, I would make a fire in our old coal stove by lighting paper first, then adding wood and finally placing some coals on top. I was not always successful the first time and the smoke and coal dust made my eyes water and my hands and face filthy. Once a week, I cleaned the house but I never enjoyed that work and was cursory about it. We didn't have a washing machine, so I learned how to wash our clothing by hand on a washboard. I rinsed the clothes under running water that was so loud I was sure no one could hear me. That's when I would sing and in those moments I was free and happy.

As part of my housekeeping duties, I had to kill a chicken if and when such was available. I would hold its feet and both of its wings with my left hand, then use my right hand to twist its neck and pluck some feathers off. I would slit the neck open with a knife, gritting my teeth and closing my eyes. The blood run quickly out of the body but if I failed to cut deeply enough, the poor bird would suddenly stand up and I would scream and jump and run away with my heart beating fast and my skin covered in goose bumps.

Besides the housework, I also cooked the family's meals, a task I grew to enjoy. I experienced the thrill of creating, marshalling the wonderful aromas and tastes. On holidays, I was soon in charge of cooking feasts for our relatives. I believed myself to be doing an excellent job and always hoped my mother would show appreciation. She did not.

One New Years, I decided to show off. I knew that my mother had invited the relatives to come for noon and in the days before I had prepared eight dishes to be served cold and three dishes to be warmed. On the morning of New Year's

1964. Shortly after Father's death.
BACK ROW: Hui Ping, Hui Min, Wei De, Hui Guo and me
FRONT : Hui Ling, Mother, Hui Li.
Hui Ling, the eldest, had just graduated from medical school and was heading to Wuhan to work as a doctor.

Day, I prepared another eight dishes to be served hot. I then went out. At 11:45, I got home to find my mother screaming at my sisters, frantically trying to organize the lunch. I feigned innocence. "What's the matter?" I asked in my calmest voice.

"Where were you?" my mother yelled. "The guests will be here at twelve. It's already 11:45!"

"I've taken care of lunch," I said, "and it will start on time." I turned to my sisters. "Excuse me, I need space to cook. Could you please leave?"

Not that there was suddenly plenty of food in China. This feast was to celebrate the Chinese New Year, and it used a whole year's carefully saved ration tickets in addition to extra tickets issued especially for New Year.

The government had meanwhile instituted a new winter heating policy dividing the country into north and south zones at the Yangtze River. Shanghai is near the mouth of the river on the south side, so the city was just inside the southern zone and was not provided with home heating, though buildings north of the river were. Our house was very cold in the winter. Every night, after cleaning my feet in a basin, I hung up a wet towel, and the next morning it would be frozen stiff. My mother slept in relative comfort with a silk and wool duvet and a bed warmer. I slept under an old cotton duvet. It didn't provide enough warmth, so I had to wear sweaters and long pants and lay my coat on top of it all. Winter was the worst time for washing clothing, since the water was so cold. My fingers would turn red and start to hurt, then become numb. I did the washing on the balcony, which was large enough for an outdoor sink and bamboo frames for drying. It was usually cold and windy, so I was in constant danger of frostbite. My round face turned purple in the wind. "Rotten Apple" unkind classmates called me.

The government controlled the supply of all consumer items in China. This included commodities such as rice, oil, meat, fish, vegetables, cotton, and coal. Within our family it was my mother who controlled access to supplies. My other four older sisters had gradually moved out of our house to attend university but Mother and my brother would often consume some treat and hide the leftovers on top of a cabinet so that Ping and I could not reach it. When I had the chance and there was no one around, I would use a stool to reach the top of the kitchen cabinet and steal—not a lot, just a small piece of meat or fish. I clearly remember once using my middle finger to scoop a chunk of peanut butter into my mouth, then shaking the bowl to smooth the surface over and hide my crime. Surprisingly, I was never caught. Sometimes, my sister and I confessed to one other in private.

Not only was the physical work hard on my small body but

my mother's behaviour towards me was overbearing and cold. After my father's death, she to rule the family just as the Qing Dynasty's famous dowager empress, Ci-Xi, had once ruled the country. Once, when I showing some hesitation in following an order, she yelled, "I am your mother, you have to obey me! Remember: if I am right, of course it is right; if I am wrong, it's still right, because I am your mother!" I felt she was treating my brother as though he was a little emperor and treating me as though I was Cinderella.

Still, life was not without its joys. One day, just as I passed a corner near our home, I heard a sound coming from behind a wall, a sound—not a voice—as though a person were screaming and crying at the same time, then moaning and groaning. The sound evoked for me someone wounded badly and in great pain, trying to move forward slowly step by step, beautiful and sorrowful at same time. I stood as though frozen, my heart caught. Later I learned that the sound I'd heard was a passage from Tchaikovsky's Violin Concerto in D major. It was played by my neighbour, a young man called Wu-Wu. From that day on, whenever I had free time, I would sneak into the little shed where he was playing his violin. When Wu-Wu found out that I was his uninvited audience and discovered how much I loved the music he played, he offered to give me free violin lessons once every two weeks if I could obtain a violin, and he told me I was welcome to come and listen to him practise any time I wanted.

I cut and sold my long hair to a wig store, collected old newspapers and empty bottles to sell to the recycling store, and collected animal parts—pig bones, squid cuttle bones, and the lining from chickens' stomachs, which I cleaned and dried before selling them to Chinese medical stores.

After six months, my fundraising efforts still fell short of my goal. Perhaps the task was too ambitious. Then suddenly an article I'd written for a country-wide magazine called *Children's Time* was published and I was paid just the amount I needed to buy a student violin. Wu-Wu lent me some sheet music so that I could painstakingly copy it by hand. For two and half years he taught me, then he left for Beijing to play in the symphony and later become a soloist. I continued to practice on my own. I was twelve years old.

At school, my status was the polar opposite of what it was at home. I was a top student, leader of my class, and a teacher's assistant. I was always appreciated and praised by the teachers and students alike. I was always given the chance to express my opinions. I was chairperson of my class all the way from Grade One to university, with the exception of the dark years that intervened. I learned that a leader is one who holds herself to a high standard in many different ways, listens to different opinions and persuades the majority to agree on the best choice. I organized many events and tried always to be helpful to others. These were the lessons my dying father had taught me.

I also enjoyed singing and dancing, though I never took any private lessons in those arts. When I was thirteen and in grade six, my choir entered the Shanghai children's choir competition. The competition was held at a sports studio, and each choir represented its school. I was in charge of conducting our choir, and was also selected to conduct the massed choirs of all the schools in the closing ceremony. We performed three popular songs, with ten thousand students involved. Music has become the work and the passion of my young life.

2 At the End of the Capitalist Road

1966-1977

In 1966 Chairman Mao proclaimed the start of the Great Proletarian Cultural Revolution. Mao wanted to solidify his power by marginalizing possible rivals Liu Shaoqi and Deng Xiaoping, but he also wanted to determine which people in the vast Party system were truly loyal to him and which were secretly followers of Liu and Deng and their latent "Capitalist Road" ideas. The Cultural Revolution was intended to uncover all of Mao's enemies in the hierarchy, from top to bottom. He could then rid himself of all the Capitalist Road—leaders like Liu and Deng as well as their followers.

I was fifteen years old and in my second year of high school, the equivalent of Canadian grade eight. I didn't really understand what the Cultural Revolution campaign was all about and didn't know how to react to it. I had only heard that Qinghua University and Beijing University were doing well in the capital by initiating "revolutionary activities." Shortly after the campaign began, Mao declared that all high school and university students in Shanghai could travel for free to Beijing to be close to the "ground zero" of the revolution.

I was excited because I'd never had the chance to travel. As soon as I heard the news I packed some clothes in my bag and left with no money in my pocket. But I had the most valuable currency with me—my student card. With the card, I could get travel arrangements for free. Because Mao was even more powerful than my mother, I didn't need to obtain her permission to go on this trip.

When I arrived at the Shanghai railway station, it was packed with students. I followed a group onto a train but waited five hours as the train remained in the station. Upon asking the reason for the delay, I was told that I was waiting on the wrong train. I left that train and ran to for the right one for my trip to Beijing. When I arrived at the train, I found that it was already crammed full of students; there was no room for even one more passenger. All spaces were occupied, including the seats, hallways, luggage racks, doorways and washrooms, but I insisted on boarding through an open window, with help from others who hoisted me up (there was no nearby platform) and pushed me in head first. I found myself lying uncomfortably on top of heads and shoulders.

After about twenty minutes and with some help, I found myself standing on my own two feet. We all waited patiently, squeezed together, until the next morning, when the train finally started to move. We were happy and excited. Some students began to cheer "Long live Chairman Mao!"

There was no food on the train, and I had brought none in my bag. Some students shared their food with me. Sometimes when the train went through a city or town at low speed, the local people would sell food through the window. Some people standing near me who had bought food shared it with me and I appreciated their generosity.

After meals, everyone needed to use the washroom. It was impossible on the train, since there were people occupying the toilets. The only opportunity came when the train stopped (it stopped and started many times without any announcement) at rural locations with no locals in sight. We tried to get out of the train through a window to urinate or have a bowel movement right there on the ground. I did my business once but only urinated because it was quick and allowed me to get back on the train safely before it pulled away. Afterwards, I saw a few students who had not finished before the train started up running to try and catch up. The train left them in the middle of nowhere. After that incident, I was too frightened of being left behind and did not leave the train again.

After three days of slow travel, we finally arrived in Beijing. My first need was a washroom, but I couldn't hold it any longer. I found a dark corner and pulled down my pants to release the contents of my bowels. At that moment my situation was so desperate that necessity trumped my embarrassment. After waiting in the station for a long time, I was sent by bus to Beijing University to stay in a dorm.

The university was a very large institution. The next day I walked around and saw a lot of large posters pasted on walls and windows, crowded on top of each other. The posters mainly criticized certain professors, calling them "Left Wing Pretender" or "Potential Capitalist." Some of the professors were accused of being America's "spies or running dogs." I also saw some strong words in support of the Cultural Revolution, such as "Down with Capitalism—up with Communism!" or "Keep the great Cultural Revolution until it succeeds" and

"Protect Chairman Mao with your own life."

When I was hungry, I went to the university's cafeteria and showed my student card, which allowed me a free meal. Although the food was served using a ladle from a huge pot, only one course daily, I still appreciated the government's generosity in providing us poor students with free meals.

After I had been in Beijing for about a week, I found out that Chairman Mao would welcome us by making an appearance at Tiananmen Square in two days. My comrades and I were very excited by the news. On Saturday afternoon, we arrived by bus at the square at one in the afternoon. I couldn't tell how many students were there, but I saw thousands of people lining up in an orderly fashion. We had been waiting for almost four hours when suddenly I heard a loud shout: "Long live Chairman Mao!" coming from my left. I saw a line of jeeps drive into the square, passing from my left to my right. Unfortunately, those jeeps were too far away and drove too fast for me to see Chairman Mao. Many people started to jump up to try to see the Great Leader. I tried it several times, but I still couldn't see him. I had been told that the Chairman would stand on a balcony at the centre of the square, allowing all of us to see him easily. Perhaps he changed his mind at the last moment for security reasons. After Chairman Mao's jeep disappeared, I was bitterly disappointed and stood crying, and at same time I heard the sound of weeping coming from all over the Tiananmen Square. Thousands of students were crying at the disappointment of missing the chance to see our "great helmsman" and hear his words.

I stayed in Beijing for about a month and visited different universities. I also went to the famous Summer Palace, which was built in the Qing Dynasty. Empress Ci-Xi had diverted the Chinese army's funds to build a beautiful, unique, and massive palace for her own summer use. Her selfish behaviour caused the Chinese army to be defeated by Britain. That at least was the reason given in our history textbook. After the defeat, Ci-Xi signed an agreement to cede parts of China to Western powers. I witnessed the massive damage to the buildings caused already by the beginning of the Cultural Revolution, but the beauty of the area was still impressive.

1966. I am fifteen and excited to be in Beijing. I hold the Little Red Book in Tien An Mien Square.

After five weeks, I decided to return to Shanghai, but transportation home was a big obstacle. I didn't want to go back by the same method as I had arrived. That train trip had left me with swollen legs for two weeks, and I remembered how I had suffered from holding my bowel movements. After pacing back and forth at the train station for a while, finding it difficult to make a decision, I finally decided to stay longer in Beijing.

I had written to sister Hui Ling upon my arrival to tell her I was staying at Beijing University, but she hadn't answered my letter. One evening, while I was sitting and reading Chairman Mao's red book in my room (I shared a room with two double beds with three other students), one of my roommates called to me from outside. "Xiao Song, you have a visitor!" (Xiao means "youth." It is a casual Chinese way to address young people.) I opened the door, and to my surprise my sister was standing there.

Hui Ling was a doctor at a hospital in Wuhan, a city up-river from Shanghai. She was temporarily stationed on the rail passenger lines to look after students who needed medical help. When she found out that I wanted to go home, she took me with her by train to Wuhan. On the way to Wuhan, I shared her sleeping car, which was a wonderful treat. I stayed in Wuhan for a week before she arranged for me to go down the Yangtze River by boat to Shanghai. While I stayed with her, she treated me very well. I felt I had finally found a mother. Since my sister didn't live in Shanghai, she promised me that she would send two renminbi per month for me and twenty renminbi per month for our mother. But as soon as the money was in Mother's hands, it was hers alone: she never gave me a penny.

When I returned to my Shanghai high school, I joined the school entertainment team. We produced musicals, mainly based on Cultural Revolutionary themes. Since I danced and sang well, it would be my way of showing support for the Cultural Revolution. I spent a lot of time rehearsing and fortunately didn't have much time to write criticisms on posters.

In the beginning, our school activities involved making posters criticizing teachers and performing some revolutionary musicals. Later, some students became more militant and joined the Red Guards. The guards were particularly rabid young Cultural Revolutionaries who banded together at Mao's instigation to fanatically promote his new ideas.

Some of the teachers were forced to confess their alleged "crimes." Then, to publicly humiliate them, the Red Guards hung signs around their necks that said "I am an American spy" or "I am a dog of capitalism" and made them wear tall, pointed cardboard hats. They were forced to walk in a circle inside the school and loudly recite the words on the signs around their necks. When the Red Guards felt that teachers weren't saying the words loudly and sincerely enough, they tortured them by forcing them into the "airplane wing" position (the guards pulled both of the teacher's arms backwards, higher and higher, until intense pain showed on their face).

My math teacher, Zhou Ying Lai, was one of the "American spies," as accused by the Red Guards. One afternoon, after our one-hour revolutionary show, the guards pushed five teachers onto the stage. All five wore the tall, pointed paper caps and huge signboards around their necks. The Red Guards shouted out their unproven crimes then ordered the five to repeat the accusations. Teacher Zhou was slapped across her face because she wasn't confessing loudly enough. When the meeting was over, my eyes met hers by accident, and I saw her anguish and humiliation. Then she quickly dropped her head. I felt sorry for her, and fought back tears. I tried to hide my feelings of sympathy and pity for her and quickly moved out of the crowd. The next morning, I heard that Teacher Zhou had hung herself in her home. She couldn't handle all those dreadful humiliations and accusations. I later heard that another teacher, Chen Wen Liang, who had been accused of being a Capitalist, had jumped off a school building to his death.

Things kept getting worse and worse. Finally, I became a target as well. First I saw a poster saying, "If some students' fathers are 'black Capitalists,' then their children cannot be clean." I knew that this referred to me. According to Chairman Mao's red book, those children could be black inside, or at least grey. Later, those students who had been born into poor families (called "reds") forced the students who had been born into rich or educated families (called "blacks") to confess their fabricated crimes.

One morning I walked into our classroom, and to my surprise saw that all the tables were gone. The benches had been divided into two sections. I was told by Red Guards to sit on the right side. At around nine thirty, the Guards announced that according to Chairmen Mao's reasoning, our class had fifteen students of the black variety and thirty-five of the red. The black students would be separated from the reds, and the black students would need to clean their dirty souls by making suitable confessions in front of the class, one by one.

I was one of the students required to make such a confession. When I looked at the faces of my classmates who were called red, I relived the good deeds I had done for them: Xiao Liu had math problems, and I had spent two hours a day doing homework with her to help her to catch up; Xiao Lee had difficulty with literature, so I'd helped her as a volunteer tutor once a week; Xiao Wong always came to school late because she had too much housework to do, so I'd even gone to her house to help her with some of the housework; and Xiao Xu, who, when we danced together, would often stand up on my leg to make a dance pose that often left me with a bruise. Now, should I confess those facts in front of the class?

Due to my "stupid and stubborn" character, which I've possessed since childhood, my confessions failed to satisfy the

Red Guards. The Guards would have liked me to say that I was a spoiled Capitalist family's princess who'd never done any real labour in my life and treated workers and red classmates badly; they would have liked me to say that I wished I could maintain my rich Capitalist lifestyle, but all those accusations were untrue. I wasn't a princess at all; I was a Cinderella who did all the dirty and heavy work at home. Every time I read my written confessions in front of the class, my voice was low and my head drooped down to my chest. It was uncomfortable and embarrassing repeating such blatant lies and slandering myself. I wished I could disappear from the classroom and drop into a deep hole, but there was nowhere for me to hide. Even though I tried my best to exaggerate any little mistake I'd made to sound like a big enough crime, my efforts didn't satisfy the Guards.

Finally, I was sent by bus with other black students to work in suburban fields doing peasant labour. The therapy of hard labour was to clean my dirty soul. After a five-hour drive, we saw large fields of golden rice waving in the wind, sight so beautiful it made me feel like dancing.

A girl named Xiao Ma and I were roommates. The room we slept in had no window, and if we closed the door, it was so dark that we couldn't see each other. "It's for your good sleep," I was told. "Dark is all you need." The room also had no beds. A local peasant woman, Wang Yu, helped us by making hay beds. She brought us a lot of dry hay and laid it on the dirt floor.

"Okay." she stood back. "This is your bed. Try to lie on it."

Xiao Ma was not too pleased at all, but I personally didn't mind. Actually, I thought it was fun sleeping on a bed of hay.

The next day, we learned how to harvest the rice crop with a sickle. We used our left hand to hold the rice near the bottom of the stalk, while the right hand held the sickle and cut the rice stalk towards the legs. At first it was awkward, but after a while I got used to it, at least until I cut my shin on the fifth day of the harvest. The cut wouldn't normally have been that serious, but because I didn't receive proper treatment, the wound became infected.

During the time my leg was infected, my job was changed to using a machine to separate the rice. The equipment reminded me of a sewing machine. I used my right foot on the bottom of the machine to make the top part roll. Then I put the top of the long rice stalk on the surface of the machine to separate the rice from the stalk. Normally, people stood up to do that job, but since my leg was hurt, I had to sit on a stool to work. It looked like it would be a very easy job until I had to hold those rice stalks over my shoulder for several days. Even though the stalks seemed light at first, they soon felt so heavy, I couldn't raise my arms.

After ten days of the rice harvest, it was time to fertilize the fields with manure. We were told to pick up the fertilizer from the big bucket by hand and spread it on the field. We went back and forth using our hands for the whole day. By the end of the day, I'd lost my appetite. It was the most awful stench I'd ever smelled in my life, and for five days I scrubbed my hands hard to try to remove it.

The three weeks of hard labour were not punishment enough for the Red Guards. At that time, nobody knew that after my father had passed away, I'd grown used to doing all kinds of manual labour at home. In fact, I'd enjoyed the fresh rural air and the earthy smell of the fields in harvest. I'd liked to walk along the narrow paths between fields in the evening humming a tune. I enjoyed being with simple, naïve peasant folk and delightful, naughty children. In some ways the hard labour forced on me by the Red Guards as a lesson was a welcome change from the chores at home.

When I returned home, I found that my school had been closed. On one hand, I was happy that I wouldn't have to confess any more, but on the other hand, I was more and more nervous that my real crimes might be discovered: my possession of a violin, copies of classical music, and my favourite novels, collected by my father in Chinese translations. *War and Peace, The Red and the Black, Pride and Prejudice, Les Misérables, Anna Karenina, Jane Eyre, Oliver Twist:* all were labelled "Capitalist poison" and if discovered by the Red Guards, they would get me into a lot of trouble. Sadly, the only solution available was to destroy all evidence of this poison. One evening as soon as the sky was dark, I sat in the backyard burning all the evidence piece by piece. Those were profoundly sad days for me, and I was quickly losing faith in our new society. Many of us were now waking up to the terrible truth of our years of brainwashing. It had taken a long time—too long—for us to see reality.

There were nine private houses in our community, together with the living quarters for a guard and his family behind a gate. Each homeowner operated their own business, and all eight owners were still alive at that time, except for my father. During that revolutionary time, we had no community guard. Red Guards began to come into our neighbours' homes as part of the Chao Jia movement, which authorized Red Guards to enter and search a private home without a search warrant and take away or destroy anything they wanted. Sometimes they would hang up or beat the homeowner when they thought that he was not cooperating. Since Red Guard groups were organized in their own schools but did not have any overall coordination, several different groups of

Red Guards could target the same black families at different times. The result was chaos.

Our neighbour, Mr. Chan, owned a fabric store. Through a window, I saw the Red Guards smashing his decorations and saw his wife kneeling down and begging. I couldn't hear what she said, but I saw the tears running down her face. On the first day, the Guards used a bicycle truck to take away a lot of fabric. On the second day I heard the sound of wood breaking. The Guards were prying up the wooden floor, hoping to try to find valuable things hidden underneath. They always suspected that homeowners were hiding things from them.

A short time later, a different group of unusually aggressive Red Guards came to the house across from ours. They started demanding that the owner, Mr. Yu, confess his crimes and volunteer to give all his valuables, including a suspected number of gold bars, to them. Later, I witnessed them tying Mr. Yu up and beating him. "Speak up!" I heard them screaming. "Tell us where the gold bars are! You're an old fox!" After three days, the Guards started digging up Yu's house and backyard. After a week of digging, I saw that the floor, walls, and backyard of his house were full of holes. I walked by quickly and pretended I hadn't seen anything.

Our whole community fell quiet and an air of depression settled on us. No one smiled or said "good morning" any more. Gradually, all of the other houses were turned upside down during visits by different groups of Red Guards.

One morning I had just returned from the market when I heard male voices in my mother's room on the second floor. I raced upstairs and saw that five Red Guards were in the room with her.

"Where's your home ownership?" one man yelled.

My mother looked nervous. "You want me to give you the

home ownership?" she asked quietly and hesitantly,

"What?" the guard cried. "You still want to keep your Capitalist house? Wake up! This is Chairman Mao's great Cultural Revolution, and everything belongs to the people!" Then I saw her slowly open a drawer and hand the ownership to the leader. Her hands were shaking. "Where are your gold and diamonds hidden?" he asked.

"I gave everything to my boss at work," she said quickly. "I have a receipt to prove it." She went to the drawer again and showed the Guard the receipt.

The leader looked at the home ownership and "donation" receipt for a few minutes, then he gave them to another guard. I was standing in the corner of the room near the door. I saw the guards looking at each other. They had finished their mission and it looked like they wanted to leave.

"Why do you need so many lamps hanging in one room?" their leader suddenly demanded. He looked around angrily. "Comrades, give the house a revolution!"

They duly set about smashing our elegant lamps and beautiful stained glass windows. As each crashed to the ground, I flinched, but I concealed my anger and stood in silence.

Years later, when my father's teacher, Zhang Tao, visited us, we found out that we had not been harassed as badly as some others during the Chao Jia movement. Teacher Zhang had protected us. He told us that Red Guards from his school knew that he had a student who had been a successful and famous Capitalist. That famous Capitalist was my father. Those Red Guards wanted to visit our home for Chao Jia, but they didn't know our address. They wanted Teacher Zhang to tell them but he insisted that he didn't know his former student's address. They became angry, tortured him and beat him then they hung him up until his arms were broken. I was sorry for what he been through on our account but I was nonetheless grateful for his protection. It was hard to imagine what might have happened if that group of angry Red Guards had come to our home.

After the Chao Jia movement, Shanghai passed into another revolutionary period called "Get Rid of the Four Olds": old ideas, old culture, old customs, and old habits. The Red Guards stood in the streets armed with scissors and knives. If they saw a woman who had kept her hair long, they would grab her by the hair and cut it short. The Guards also used knives to make "corrections" to your clothes. If they saw somebody wearing colourful or tight clothing, they would cut the clothing to make sure that it couldn't be worn any longer. If you wore high-heeled shoes, they would use their knives to cut the heels off.

On some streets, the Red Guards piled up coffins, violins, and classic books taken from people's homes during the Chao Jia movement and burned them in the street. I had already burned my violin and novels in secret and was glad not to suffer this humiliation publicly.

I saw an old woman crying and screaming as her coffin was burned in the street. She believed that when she died, the coffin would take her to heaven. Now she didn't care if her screaming brought further persecution. A lot of people had stopped and were watching in sympathy, but all were too frightened to stop the Red Guards.

Soon the cemeteries were in chaos. The Guards were destroying "black" people's remains. We rushed to the cemetery to pick up Father's ashes and return them to our home. At first we couldn't find his remains in their regular place but after a long search we found them in the back corner of the cemetery grounds. We saw that many others had already been destroyed, and some funerary boxes were broken, the ashes spilled everywhere. We took up my father's box and my moth-

Father's first grave was in his brother's backyard in a suburb of Wuxi. The new grave is in a suburb of Shanghai.

er stored his ashes in my bedroom.

That's when I at last learned my father's family secret. He had been born into an impoverished family in a small village, a suburb of Wuxi city. His parents had arranged for him to be adopted for a fee by a family who were unable to have their own child. They lived in Ningbo, a few hours' drive from Shanghai. From there he had engineered his brilliant rise to prosperity. His foster parents and his birth parents had both passed away before his death, but his brothers were still alive. Since they were exceptionally poor, they were designated as Reds during the Cultural Revolution. My mother decided that the house of one of the red brothers would be a safe place to keep the ashes. We carried them to Wuxi, to Father's third brother's house, and the third brother buried my father's ashes in his backyard. He refused to put my father's name on the grave, because he had been a Capitalist. This was very hurtful. I swore an oath to my father in my heart: Father, one day I will rebury you properly and put your name on the grave marker in big characters. I love you; I miss you, my father.

3 Blood Pressure

1967-1975

Since all schools were closed in 1967, we students had to spend our time participating in revolutionary programs in our local community.

Every day at eight A.M. and six P.M., the Red Guards would make us assemble at our community centre and stand with our faces to the wall, on which Chairman Mao and Vice Chairman Lin Biao's portraits were posted. Liu Shaoqi was no longer a Vice Chairman because of his alleged Capitalist crimes, so Mao had picked Lin Biao to be Vice Chairman. Lin Biao controlled the army and faithfully supported the Cultural Revolution. He was always seen in public clutching Mao's little red book of wise sayings. At these student gatherings, we all waved the red book and chanted three times "Long live Chairman Mao and best wishes to Vice Chairman Lin Biao's good health." The eight A.M. gatherings were termed "the morning greetings" and those at six P.M. were "the evening reports." Every afternoon at one P.M. we assembled in the community meeting room to study Mao's book for two hours to further our understanding of the Great Proletarian Cultural Revolution.

After the Chao Jia movement, the government decreed that other poor families would move into our house. A family with four children moved into our house, occupying our first floor and paying a low rent to the local government. The house right across from ours became home to five families. Our community, from its original nine families, ballooned to twenty-one, all living in those same nine houses. The government also took away our gate and guard.

My job—running our household and doing all of the housework—continued through this period. One day while I was washing the family's clothing and singing on the open balcony, I noticed a young man watching me from a window across from our house. His gaze embarrassed me, and I blushed and stopped singing. From that day on, I frequently noticed that same young man watching me from his room. I learned that he was one of our new neighbours, and that his name was Fa Ling.

Our community had twelve teenagers, four boys and eight girls. Fa Ling was the one boy that all the young girls considered to be attractive. He liked to tell funny stories to make them laugh and would get their attention by playing tunes on a bamboo flute. He also liked to show off his impressive bicycling skills, and often he would take a girl for a ride, she sitting behind him. Most of the girls gathered outside eagerly, waiting for the chance to be chosen for one of these bicycle rides. When Fa Ling showed up, the girls would open their arms and scream, "My turn! Pick me up!" I was the only girl who kept her distance; I sat and watched from a distance. When Fa Ling offered me a ride, I always declined and left.

He knew that I was keeping my distance and acting cool

towards him, but I couldn't understand why he still paid a lot of attention to me, treating me as though I was more special than the others. On one hand, I felt nervous and shy, so I was even more cool and distant towards him, but on the other, it felt good to be chased by such a popular young man. This continued for about six months.

One night, after leaving a party at my friend Kang May's home, Fa Ling and I walked home together in the dark. When we reached my house, I opened the door to say goodbye to him. Just before I went inside, Fa Ling suddenly grabbed my hand and gently kissed it. I felt as though electricity were passing through my body, my heart was beating so fast. I was frozen at the door for a few seconds, then I went quickly into the house and closed the door. That incident at the door was the beginning of our platonic love.

It was now the autumn of 1967. I was sixteen years old and was supposed to have graduated from my junior high school ("Zhu-Zhong" in Chinese), and in that same year my brother, who was now nineteen, should have graduated from his senior high school ("Gao-Zhong" in Chinese). In the fall, both of us were summoned to our schools to discuss our graduations.

We learned that during the Cultural Revolution, the government had introduced new rules for the students who had recently graduated from high school:

1. No students would be going on to the next level of education.
2. All graduated students must go to work.
3. The work locations were to be divided between two areas:
   a) We would work in city of Shanghai, or
   b) We would work as a peasant anywhere in China that they cared to send us.

   This relocation policy was called "Shang Shan-Xia

Xiang," literally meaning "go up to the mountain, down to the village."

4. If a family only had one student graduating, the work assignment would depend on the student's family colour. The reds could stay in Shanghai and get a job. The blacks must go "Shang Shan-Xia Xiang" and work in the fields as a peasant.
5. If a family had two red students graduating at the same time, both were allowed to have jobs in Shanghai. For black families, one was allowed to work in Shanghai, but the other must be assigned "Shang Shan-Xia Xiang."
6. If a student had severe health problems, he or she could wait until their health improved. Then the government would find them a suitable job.

Our teachers allowed the students a week to discuss the situation with their families before coming back to school for the final decision. I reported the policy to my mother, hoping that we could discuss it. "It's obvious," she sniffed. "You know what you should do, don't you?"

My brother was the prince who deserved to stay in Shanghai. I would have to give up living in the city and go far away to work as a peasant.

My boyfriend Fa Ling was the same age as me and was facing graduation too. Since he was born into a working-class family, he was labelled a red and would stay in Shanghai. I knew that the graduation would mean we had to part. I was sad, but this was my fate and there was no point complaining about it.

Then, to my great surprise, Fa Ling announced that he would go anywhere and work in the fields, as long as he could be with me.

"Are you crazy?" I looked at him without smiling. "You'd

give up the opportunity to stay in the big city with a good job? No, please don't do that!"

But he insisted that we could be happy together in the country. Hard physical labour was not daunting to him, as long we would be together. He told me I was the only person that he would ever love. He also said he would marry me as soon as our age qualified us, according to government rules. I was deeply moved, and without any more words, I kissed him and hugged him and my heart went to him. Our relationship changed from platonic love to a physical one at that moment. I had no reason to hold back from him any more. I wanted to give him as much as I could, without having sex. At that time in China, any woman of value would keep her virginity until after marriage, as we had all been taught.

After a week, Fa Ling and I returned to our own schools, and we both told our classes, "I have decided to go Shang Shan-Xia Xiang." We were surprised when Fa Ling became a hero. A newspaper published a story about him, describing how a great student had followed Chairman Mao's "Shang Shan-Xia Xiang" directions, being willing to give up a good urban job to do peasant's work, a great student who loved Mao more than himself. The government organized many appearances for him, unaware that his real motivation was to follow me.

While Fa Ling was busy making speeches at different schools, I hardly saw him. His biggest appearance was in a sports stadium in front of ten thousand people. It was the same stadium in which I had conducted the school choir four years earlier. This time, not were only those ten thousand students listening to his speech, but his voice was broadcast to the whole country. That day I sat at home with a small portable radio and listened to every word. Although I knew the reason why he had given up the chance to stay in Shanghai, and it was not the one he gave in his speech, I was terribly excited and proud of him.

The speeches kept Fa Ling busy for about three months, but finally they came to an end. It gave me a chance to discuss our choice of a place to go, from the lists at the school. But he told me that the government had already made the decision for him. He would stay in Shanghai and start working at the railway station in two weeks. Now he wanted me to stay in the city too.

"How?" I asked.

"Don't worry, Hui Zhi. I've come up with a plan for you."

His plan was that I would claim I had high blood pressure and couldn't do hard labour. Then I would be able to stay in Shanghai with him.

"But I don't have high blood pressure," I said.

"You'll need to give yourself high blood pressure, my dear," he said, and he took a small paper bag from his pocket. Inside were some small white pills. "If you take a pill, after half an hour your blood pressure will rise temporarily."

I knew that this was dishonest, but I accepted it anyway. I told myself that I was fortunate to have someone who loved me deeply and would do anything for me. This was the only way that we would be able to stay together. Still, from the very beginning, I was nervous about it. I tried taking the pills several times, and each time when I went to the local clinic to have my blood pressure checked, it had risen to 140 over 90. I was confident that I could go to school and claim that due to high blood pressure, I needed to stay home and rest.

After I showed my high blood pressure report to school officials, they ordered me to go back to the hospital from time to time to have it checked out, accompanied by a teacher.

Sometimes this doubtful teacher came without notice to my home to take me to hospital and I had to swallow the pill before I left the house. One morning about seven thirty, on a day when I didn't need to go to the market, I had just got out of bed when I heard a commotion outside. Looking out, I saw a team of Red Guards standing at our front door

"Follow Chairman Mao's orders to Shang Shan-Xia Xiang! Shame on those staying home! Long live Chairman Mao!" Some held red flags and some loudly beat drums and gongs.

I knew they had come for me. My heart started beating fast and my hands shook. I rushed into the washroom and quickly swallowed three pills. I was worried that one would not be enough to make my blood pressure rise in such a short time. After a few minutes, I heard heavy footsteps on the stairs. "Oh my god, they're coming," I thought. I heard my heart beat so loudly that it felt as though it was almost coming out of my throat.

"How are you today, Xiao Song?" my teacher asked.

"I'm fine," I mumbled.

"Today is your lucky day. We have invited a doctor to give you a house call and check your blood pressure. First, let our Red Guards read one of Chairman Mao's quotations with you."

I slowly opened Mao's quotation book and started reading along with the Red Guards, but I felt dizzy and nauseous. I don't remember how long it took, but the doctor finally noticed my face turning pale, and that I was sweating profusely. He told me to lie down and measured my blood pressure. It was dangerously high: 160 over 120. It was far too high for a sixteen-year-old girl.

Soon afterwards, I developed a genuine high blood pressure problem and my kidneys stopped functioning properly.

The authorities didn't bother checking my blood pressure any more, but I started to worry about my health. I took medication to lower it and also began to learn tai-chi and chi-gong. These traditional Chinese arts were later to prove of great benefit to me.

In 1968, Ping, who was fifteen, graduated from junior high school and was sent to Jilin province, on the border of North Korea, to start her difficult journey through life.

Since I had technically agreed to "Shang Shan-Xian Xiang," in 1967 my brother was to have been given a job in Shanghai, as Mother had wished. Unfortunately, she worried too much about him. She did not want him to be a labourer in a factory, so she told him to write "I used to have a heart problem and arthritis" on the job application. She thought the excuse would help him obtain an office job but the claim was to give the school a great pretext to not give him any job at all, since he was from a Capitalist family.

After more than a year of staying idly at home, he grew bored with his situation. The government had no intention of giving him a job in Shanghai, so he went to Anhui province and worked in the fields without being compelled to. My eldest sister, Hui Ling, was a doctor in the city of Wuhan and my second sister, Hui Li, was a teacher in a small city in Shanxi province in the northwest of China. My third sister, Hui Guo, was an accountant in Guilin in the southwest of China, and the fourth, Hui Min, was an engineer in Taiyaun, the capital of Shanxi province.

Now only my mother and I lived alone in the house in Shanghai. Fa Ling and I continued our relationship until my mother caught us kissing in the darkness of our kitchen.

"Never, ever come to my home again!" she shouted. "If you come here again with your right leg, I will break your right leg! If you come into my house with your left leg, I will break your left leg!" Then she turned to me. "You are not allowed to date this man! He was born into a working class family, and his whole family is squashed together on one floor. He's looking for the chance to live at my house and take my property away! I don't want you to see him any more!"

I stood in silence, but I could never agree with her suspicions. I believed that true love came from the heart and had nothing to do with poverty or wealth. I thought of a story I'd read in an elementary school textbook about a poor Western couple who had no money to buy Christmas presents. The husband had a watch without a chain; the wife had long, beautiful hair but no comb. The husband sold his watch to buy a comb for his wife, and his wife sold her long hair to buy a watch chain for her husband. On Christmas day, they gave each other the presents and discovered that the gifts were not useful any more, but the love they felt for each other grew even deeper and stronger. I believed that the feelings between Fa Ling and I were on the same level. Material things did not matter to us.

Fa Ling still played his flute; we decided to use it as a secret signal. He played different songs, chosen as signals, such as: "There is nobody at my home, I want you to come over," or "I am free to meet you outside," or "Don't come to my home, the situation has changed." Every night he would stand in the street just outside my window playing for me. I fell asleep with that peaceful music surrounding me, and I felt that I was the luckiest woman in the world.

Once, when my period didn't come at the usual time, I became worried that I might be pregnant, even though I hadn't had any real sexual contact with him. When I was growing up, no one had told me about sex and reproduction. I was only told in high school biology class that when a female's egg meets a male's sperm, the cell could develop into a baby. That little piece of knowledge gave my imagination a lot of room for speculation. I thought pregnancy could occur from washing his clothes. I imagined that if I got the semen from his underwear on my hands when I went to the bathroom and cleaned myself, it might somehow meet my ovum and produce a baby.

At that time, if a girl got pregnant before marriage, she would be ostracized. Her school would expel her, and if she had a job, the company would fire her. Many girls committed suicide because of unwanted pregnancies. I was nervous and ashamed of my situation. I took some Chinese herbal medicine labelled "forbidden pregnancy," which was supposed to increase blood circulation. At the same time, I pushed my belly hard to try to get rid of my imagined "baby." Eventually, of course, my period did come, because I was still a virgin.

Fa Ling's remaining family lived on the second floor of the building across from our house. His father worked in a factory, and his mother had retired early due to illness. He had four sisters and two brothers. The three older sisters were married and no longer lived with their family. The family had divided one big room into three small rooms on the second floor. Fa ling shared a small room with his brother. Since he worked at the Shanghai railway station six days a week, and I didn't have a job, I visited him at his house every morning just after shopping at the food market when my mother was still in bed, and he continued to play for me in the street every night. On some Sundays he would take me out to dinner. To avoid Mother, we always communicated through his flute. We lived so close that we could see each other through our windows. The whole community knew of our relationship;

most people called us "the little couple." His family always welcomed my visits.

After we had dated for about two years, Fa Ling was moved to another department at work, and his hours became irregular. One afternoon while he was at work, I went to his home to wash his clothes. I put his clothes in a big wooden washbasin, then I took it to the washing board to clean the clothing piece by piece. While soaping his pants, I felt something in one of the pockets. It was a folded piece of paper. It was already wet. I felt guilty for not checking all of the pockets before I started washing, so I put the paper on the window glass to carefully dry it, but at same time I read the contents.

> My darling Fa Ling, I cannot stop myself from thinking about you. The time we spend together made me so happy: your touch, your smell just made me crazy. Although I know Hui Zhi is your formal girlfriend, I know you want me too…
> Yours
> Lee Ping

I couldn't believe my eyes. At first my head felt so frozen that I couldn't feel or think for a few minutes, then as the shock wore off, the pain began. I ran home to my bedroom and started crying. I cried for a long time then lay on my bed and pondered. Finally, I reached a decision. I wrote to him: "I don't want to have an unfaithful boyfriend like you. You have hurt me. Goodbye." Then I put my letter on top of Lee Ping's in one envelope and took it to Fa Ling's house, placing the envelope underneath his pillow. I didn't sleep well that night. All of our time together flashed through my head as though I were watching a movie.

Fa Ling continued to send musical signals that he wanted

1969

My boyfriend Fa Ling let me use his bike and took this photo for me. I was 18 years old.

to meet me, but I did not respond. Early one Sunday morning, when I was on my way to the market, I saw him waiting for me. He tried to explain that he had no feelings for that girl. He loved only me. He said that the relationship had started with flirting. He admitted that he had made a mistake by giving in to his weakness for sex. He promised again and again that it would never be repeated. Finally I accepted his apology.

Five months later, I found another damaging letter, from a different girl. I was incensed, and after a big fight, I told him that our relationship was over for good.

After I broke up with him, he followed me everywhere and did his best to convince me to change my mind. Occasionally when I was on my way home late at night and nearing my house, he would come out from the dark and surprise me.

Our washroom windows faced each another. We could see and hear each other clearly, and most of the time our washroom windows were left open with their curtains half open to let in the air. Every time I wanted to use our washroom, I had to check to see whether he was at home. If he was there, I had to sneak into the washroom and quickly pull the curtain to fully cover the window. If he saw me, he would try to get my attention. He also continued with the musical signals. His obsessive attentions were bothering me so much that I felt I had no freedom any more. At the same time, I worried that I would weaken and go back to him. That possibility frightened me. Finally, against my better judgment, I decided to ask for my mother's help.

It was a beautiful sunny Sunday afternoon when I finally screwed up the courage to go to her room.

"Mother, please help me. Fa Ling has hurt me too much, and I don't want to see him or hear from him any more. But he is following me everywhere I go. I don't know what I can do and how I can get rid of him. I need your help. What can I do to stop him?" I kneeled before her and started crying, begging her for guidance. "Please help me, Mother."

She stared at me a moment. "What do you want us to do?"

she asked. "Move for you? You're an unwanted child, do you know that? You deserve to suffer because you didn't listen to me in the beginning."

Her cold voice and hurtful words felt like a bucket of freezing water over my head. I stopped crying. I slowly got up and left her room. I felt shame for having wept in front of her. From that moment forward, the remoteness of our relationship deepened forever. I hardly ever spoke to her and received her orders with a simple "yes."

In 1970, at the Chinese New Year, none of my five sisters had enough money to come home for the holidays, but my brother did, because Mother had sent money to him. I cooked all the dishes as usual and set three bowls of rice on the table. After my brother finished his first, he pointed at his empty bowl and ordered me to fill it up. "The rice pot is just behind you," I pointed out to him. "You can fill it up yourself."

My mother slapped me. "I feel miserable, and you make me feel even worse!" she shouted. She hit me hard on the head with her chopsticks. "I don't want to celebrate New Year any more!" she screamed. She smashed the dishes, still filled with food, on the floor. I understood that she was disappointed about her son leaving home, but it wasn't my fault. I had already given up a job in Shanghai for my brother's sake. Regardless, when he went to Anhuai to work in the fields, it still hadn't helped me get a job in Shanghai.

Although I knew that I was Mother's unwanted child, I had never received any physical abuse from her until that day. I didn't cry, I just held my swollen face and left.

In my room, I broke down. "I hate you!" I cried. "I hate you both!" I covered my head with a blanket. After that day I refused to eat with them, and I never showed my emotions in front of them again.

Chapter Three

I started to write letters to my dead father. "Dear Father, please tell me if the mother I have is my true birth mother. Why doesn't she love me and protect me? Why does she treat me like Cinderella?" Or "Father, why is the whole world so upside down? Why don't people follow basic ethics? Why does our great leader Chairman Mao let Red Guards do these destructive things that even kindergarten kids recognize as wrong?" or "My dear Father, why are the lessons I learned in school and from you no longer useful? I really don't understand my mother, my family and my country. Where are my future and my hope? What am I living for?"

I folded each letter carefully and stored them in a cardboard box. I would keep the box underneath my pillow and fall asleep feeling close to my father.

I started to feel that I should never have been born and became increasingly emotional. I often walked the half hour to the Huang-Po river ferry and paid the three cents fare to get over to the other side to the district called Pudong. Pudong was nearly vacant at that time, and it was easy to find a place to be alone. It gave me a chance to release my sadness without anyone seeing me. Sometimes I would stand at the end of the ferry and look down at the muddy yellow water flowing slowly on its way to the East China Sea. Gradually, in the depth of my contemplation, I forgot the whole world and myself. After an hour's daydreaming, someone would call out to me, "Hi, little comrade, time is up. We are closing the boat." Sometimes, on rainy days, when I saw rain lashing down, I would run outside until I was soaking wet to cool the fire inside my chest.

My bedroom was located between the first and second floors. It was nicknamed the "Pagoda Room" but was only six by eight feet, with room only for a bed, a table and a chair. The floor was cement, and the two small windows were broken. It was hot in the summer and extremely cold in the winter. One day I found three books I had neglected to burn: an art book with photos of Michelangelo's paintings, a second art book with photos of Raphael's art, and a third, a biography of a famous Russian ballet dancer. When I'd finished my housework, I would joyfully lock myself in my little bedroom to read those three books but also to copy the two famous painters' works. I had now taken up residence in my own spiritual world and I drew some comfort and sense of peace from my pencil and watercolours.

One night, when I was about to go to bed, I was startled to discover Fa Ling sitting on my bed. I controlled my voice to keep it low. "Are you crazy?" I whispered. "How did you get into my bedroom?"

"From outside. I climbed the wall and came in through the broken window."

"What do you want?"

"I want to talk to you," he said. "I still love you, Hui Zhi, and want you to come back to me."

"I've already told you I don't want to be your girlfriend."

An argument ensued. I was afraid that if I kept him in my room any longer and my mother noticed, then the fireworks would really start. To avoid this, I agreed to talk to him the next morning at his house. I made sure he left my room safely through the window and got down to the ground. I didn't sleep well that night. Why, if he loved me so much that he would take the risk of falling, would he be constantly be unfaithful? I mulled it over all night, but I couldn't come up with a good answer.

The next day at ten in the morning, I went over to his home as agreed. It was very quiet because there was no one else around. I learned that a relative had passed away, and his whole family had gone to the funeral. He'd made an excuse as to why he couldn't go with them. Now I understood why he'd taken such a risk in climbing into my room the night before—it was to take advantage of this rare opportunity to be alone with me.

First he handed me a letter. It was addressed to Lee Ping. It said that he had never loved her and wanted to end their relationship. He told me again how much he loved me and how difficult it was for him to live without me. He admitted that he had a weakness for womanizing, and he believed that only I could help him, because he saw so many more good qualities in me than he saw in others.

It was a very difficult decision. I still had feelings for him, but how much could he really change? Could I trust him again? I didn't know. I told him my feelings, then he told me that if I accepted his offer of engagement and agreed to marry him, he would help me start violin lessons again, including buying me a new violin and paying for my lessons. I was so taken aback that I didn't know what to say to him. Of course, I wanted to be loved and wanted to continue my musical education in hopes of one day becoming a professional musician. But Fa Ling added the condition that if he did all of this for me, I would have to give up my virginity to him to demonstrate my commitment. It would help him develop the resolve, he said, the resolve to try harder to rid himself of his weakness.

At age nineteen, it was one of the most difficult decisions I'd had to make. In the end, I lost my virginity to him, though I didn't enjoy this first painful sexual experience at all. Afterwards, I regretted my poor decision, knowing that it ran against my basic principles of right and wrong. I had been taught that a virtuous woman should keep her virginity until she is married, or else sex will be a dirty poison for her soul. We were all unaware that our country's virtuous leader, Mao Zedong, was secretly having all the promiscuous sex he wanted.

Fa Ling was happy—he'd got what he wanted. After the meeting and sex with me, he went out and bought a lot of food, and that night I ate at his house with his family. I didn't care whether my mother noticed my absence. During the dinner, Fa Ling announced that we had just become engaged. His mother gave me a house key, and she said that I could visit any time I wanted, even if there was no one at home.

By this time, the Cultural Revolution had been going for nearly five years, and Mao's wife Jiang Qing was now in charge of China's national entertainment policy. She changed the Chinese opera's agenda to revolutionary performances containing themes about the civil war between Mao and Chiang Kai-shek, operas that all ended joyously with Mao's victory. The symphony stopped playing Western classical music, switching instead to music by Chinese composers such as the "Yellow River Piano Concerto." She still allowed ballet performances, but classical ballet was replaced by a revolutionary type.

Jiang Qing commissioned a famous ballet called The White-Haired Girl. It describes a poor family in which the father has borrowed some money from his landlord. At Chinese New Year, the landlord demands that the father pay it back, or his home will be forfeited. When he doesn't have enough money to pay back the loan, the father commits suicide. His daughter escapes to live in the wilderness for eighteen years. She survives by eating wild animals and fruit, and her long hair turns and pure white. One stormy night, she returns to the village and the landlord sees her as a ghost. In the end, she kills the landlord and joins Mao's Red Army.

China still needed musicians, those who could play Chinese instruments and those who played Western ones. This gave me hope they would find a place for me one day. Because there were too many violinists in Shanghai, I thought that if I changed from violin to cello, it would provide more opportunities. I loved the cello's deep and sad sound, which seemed to fit perfectly into my own sorrowful life.

I started learning to play the cello shortly after my engagement to Fa Ling. It brought excitement and energy into my life. My cello teacher, Pan Lang, played with the Shanghai Ballet Company. Since Jiang Qing's revolutionary changes, the company had not been able to put on as many performances and the ballet was not bringing in enough money. Pan Lang starting teaching private lessons and came to my home once a week.

Teacher Pan always arrived with written sheet music and left copies for me to practise with during the week. Since I didn't need to spend time hand-copying sheet music I could concentrate fully on practising. I locked myself in my tiny bedroom to practise five to six hours a day. After a year or so, Teacher Pan declared that I had developed the ability to learn more difficult pieces. He started giving me more homework, including pieces he was playing in his own performances. I was excited to have the opportunity to learn more and to learn faster. When it was time to learn how to shift the fingering position on the cello from first to second and third, my fingers would bleed until calluses developed, but I didn't pay any attention to the pain. Once, Teacher Pan lent me a record of Swan Lake and a record player. He warned me that, according to Jiang Qing's rulings, the piece was considered

Capitalist poison. I would have to be careful not to let the neighbours hear. If someone reported my crime, I promised never to confess that the music had come from him. By the time Teacher Pan took the Swan Lake record back, I could hum Tchaikovsky's entire ballet from beginning to end by heart.

I spent most of 1972 practising, but on one of these routine days, a major event took place that affected all of the citizens of Shanghai. The president of the United States, Richard Nixon, arrived in our city for his groundbreaking seven-day visit to China.

I didn't know how to react to this surprising news, since China had closed its doors to the West for so long. We had become accustomed to our isolation from the non-Communist world. We had already heard that Nixon would visit China between February 21 and 28, and the first day would be in Shanghai, because on February 14, our local party officials ordered that one person from each family should attend an emergency meeting to prepare for the event. My mother told me to go. During the meeting, I learned that our government had ordered our entire population to stay at home on the 21st. In addition to having to remain indoors, we were forbidden to hang any laundry if it would be visible from the street and to open any window that faced onto a street. We could only guess at the reason, but I believed that these strict measures were to prevent any possible breaches of security and to hide any signs of dissent. It also made the city look clean.

On February 21st, a guard was sent to stay in our home from seven thirty A.M. to five thirty P.M. to make sure that we followed the orders. There was a lot of tension in the air, but I grew bored and asked if I could practice my cello. The guard denied my request, so I just read a book and slept the whole afternoon to pass that "special" day. Later I heard that Nixon's visit was successful, but I will never forget how one of world's biggest cities became a ghost town for that day in order that the Americans would not see the truth.

After nearly four years of concentrated, determined effort on the cello, my teacher decided that because I already had the foundation of a few years of playing violin, and because of my great patience and hard work, my skills were at a level that most cellists could only achieve after six years of practice. I could apply to symphonies in some small cities in poorer provinces, such Lanzhou, but I was not yet good enough for a big city like Shanghai or Beijing. I was considering his advice about applying to the Lanzhou symphony, in the north on the Yellow River. Suddenly I received the astonishing news that our government was offering me work in a local factory.

Although I loved playing music and desperately wanted to be a cellist, I sorely needed a job so that I could become more independent, and I also had to consider that my fiancé lived in Shanghai as well. I decided to accept the job in the factory and hoped that after my lifelong financial dependence on my mother and our poor relationship, my trying experiences would be left behind.

Two months after I started work, Fa Ling came down with pulmonary tuberculosis. He was sent to a hospital. He needed an injection every day and lots of rest to control the disease. Sadly, he was released from hospital after only a week, but the reason was a real shock to me. During the week in the hospital, he had made sexual advances to the nurses, and two of them had reported it to their supervisors. I couldn't believe his behaviour, but since he was ill, and I was his fiancée, I still believed that it was my responsibility to help him. He needed the injection daily, but he refused to go back to the same hospital for it. The hospital was free only for railway employees. He could go to a local hospital to get the required injection, but he would have to pay. He refused to go. Since it was very a dangerous situation for him without medication, the only option was for me to give him the needed injections.

I bought a medical book and learned how to perform the injection, then I practiced on my thigh with vitamin doses. It took me three days of practice before I felt confident enough to perform the task. Every day after I finished work in the factory, I came home to administer the medication. I also lent him many inspirational books, hoping he would develop some good qualities from reading those heroic stories. After about a year of medication and rest at home, Fa Ling's health finally improved. He started to work for half a day doing light work for the railway. He believed that I had saved his life, but unfortunately, he couldn't save himself.

One afternoon, after I had finished all of the housework, I went over to Fa Ling's house. He wasn't at home, and his brother told me that he might be at Aunty Ting's place, since he had recently been paying her frequent visits. Aunty Ting was called "aunt" though she was not related to Fa Ling. In the Chinese custom, people can be called "Sister," or "Aunt" or "Grandma," depending on their age, as a matter of politeness. She was an attractive thirty-six-year-old with two children. Her husband had been sentenced to jail for three years after being convicted of stealing. Her whole family lived in a six-by-eight-foot room, the same size as my own bedroom. The room was between the first and second floor of Fa Ling's home.

Aunty Ting had the reputation of being a prostitute. Suspicious, I walked down the six steps and knocked on the door. It wasn't locked and was opened with a gentle push. I saw Fa Ling and Aunty Ting lying on the bed. I screamed and ran away.

I would not tolerate any more excuses or promises from him. I knew it would be impossible for me to share my life with him. I broke the relationship off by refusing to see him or talk to him. I think he finally realized there was no hope and that I could no longer forgive him. Two weeks later, I was washing clothes on our balcony. Through his half-covered window, I saw him having sex with two girls at the same time. I strongly felt that he was allowing me to see this intentionally to send me a message: "Look, you didn't want to be with me any more, so are you happy to see me sinking lower and lower?"

It made me feel terrible seeing him behaving like an animal. I also felt bad for myself in that I hadn't been strong enough to leave him much earlier. Less than a year after this, two detectives visited me at my factory. They wanted to know the details of my relationship with Fa Ling at the time I had been dating him. At first I refused to provide information. I believed that my relationship wasn't anyone's business, and I found it highly embarrassing when they asked questions of a sexual nature. Then they explained that police had received reports from many parents about Fa Ling hurting their daughters. He was using dating to entice young girls into sex. After finishing with one victim, he would move on to another. The police told me that this was a crime and had to be investigated. They'd heard I was Fa Ling's long-term girlfriend and had broken off the relationship because of his infidelities. They wanted to know how many other women Fa Ling had been sexually involved with during the time I was with him. I told the detectives the truth, as far as I knew it. He was arrested and sent to jail.

Our relationship had lasted eight long years. I was now twenty-four years old and no longer that naïve teenager watching Fa Ling showing off his cycling skills. I was ready to move on.

4 The Good Engineer

1973–1985

In September 1973, when I was twenty-two, I started working at a factory that produced carburetors for small cars and motorcycles. Of the five hundred employees, about eighty percent were illiterate. I started by working in the department that assembled all of the separate parts into a whole carburetor. After a half year with a good work record, my job was changed to repairing failed carburetors. Usually the failures were caused by someone assembling them incorrectly in the first place or with unsuitable parts. My salary was thirty-three renminbi per month with a three renminbi bonus if my supervisors thought I was a hard and capable worker. My salary was thus the equivalent of eight U.S. dollars. I worked a lot of overtime, especially when the factory was rushing to supply an order on time and many carburetors still needed repairs to complete the order. Each overtime hour worked was recorded on a time card. The management allowed me to claim equivalent time off when I needed it.

Since I'd started work, I was no longer able to cook meals

at home. We were back to buying food from the local cafeteria again, but this food was bland and cost more. Fortunately, my mother had retired from the post office a month and a half after I started work. She was fifty five and had never cooked one meal in her whole life. This was a good time for her to learn. However, she soon developed the habit, after cooking a meal, of taking the better part of the food for herself and leaving the worst part for me, who had contributed half of my salary. I may have been supporting myself but my situation at home hadn't changed.

I rose every morning at five A.M. to shop at the market. I would go home and prepare the ingredients for Mother to cook later. I rode my bicycle to the park to do tai-chi and qi-gong for an hour before going to work. I often stopped to buy a bun while I was cycling and went home for lunch, since we had a one-hour break: twenty minutes for the return trip, ten minutes for lunch, and thirty minutes for a nap. Every evening I would practice the cello for two to three hours before going to bed. Each Sunday, after I had worked for six days, I had to clean the whole house, wash all of our clothes, and cook the meals. For the first two years, before we broke up, I also spent some time with Fa Ling. I was always in a rush and there never seemed to be time enough for me to do all the things I wanted to.

In the summer of 1974, in my second year of work, my third sister, Hui Guo, came home to deliver twins. She was an accountant in Guilin, a province in the southwest. Since Shanghai had better quality doctors and hospitals, and it was her birthplace, she decided to return home for her first delivery. Her husband couldn't come to Shanghai—he had to stay and work, especially given that they would have twins to look after. In response to China's high birthrate, the government had instituted a one-child policy, though if a mother had twins, it was considered a natural exception.

Mother let my sister, Hui Guo, sleep on the third floor, since our first floor was currently occupied by another family due to the policies of the Cultural Revolution. I still slept in the little Pagoda Room and Mother used the second floor with the biggest bedroom and its attached washroom. On the night of the fifth day after my sister's arrival, I was wakened by the sound of screaming. I ran to my sister's room and saw a lot of water on her bed and floor. Since I didn't know what had happened, I had to ask Mother to help. She told me to call an ambulance. We didn't have a telephone at home but used the telephone service station located about five minutes walk away. The phone service station was open from eight A.M. to eight P.M. every day, but it was now eleven, and I didn't know where I could make a call.

First I went to the telephone station, hoping that someone had forgotten to lock the door, but it wasn't so. Then I thought of the only place that could still be open and have telephones, the police station. I ran to our local police station, but fear stopped me at the front door. I had never entered a police station in my life, and the policemen I'd seen before were always yelling at someone. I paced back and forth in front of the station for about twenty minutes until a policeman came out and yelled at me. "Hey! What are you doing here?"

"I…I'm looking for a phone to call an ambulance. My sister needs to deliver her baby." They allowed me to make the call from the station.

The ambulance arrived at about midnight, and Mother and I accompanied my sister to the hospital. When we got to the admitting desk, my sister was sent to the emergency room right away, while we remained in the waiting room.

After about an hour, a doctor came out and spoke to Mother. "Your daughter has to deliver twins. Her water breaking could cause the babies to die inside her womb. She needs to deliver them right away. We tried to help her to deliver them in a natural way, but it has failed. We found out that one baby is in the wrong position inside the womb. We need to operate to bring the babies out. It will be a risk and we need a family member to sign a release paper before the operation." Then the doctor handed an agreement to Mother to sign.

Mother didn't take the agreement. She pointed to me. "You sign the paper!"

I took the paper and read it. It said that the person who agreed to allow the doctors to perform an operation was taking on the risk—even if death resulted. Although I was nervous about taking on such a big responsibility, I realized that time was running out and I needed to save my sister's and her babies' lives. I signed my name and suddenly felt that I had grown ten years older.

Mother went home to bed after I signed the agreement, while I remained, waiting. Eventually I fell asleep on the bench.

I woke up with a doctor shaking me. "Hey! Wake up. Your sister just delivered two boys!"

I jumped up. "How are they doing?"

"They are all fine. You can come inside to see her." I walked into the room and saw that my sister's face was very pale and tired, but the babies had been taken away already. She told me that she had lost a lot of blood and that the doctor would give her a transfusion. She also told me that one of her twins had sustained a small injury on the surface of his head during the delivery. The twins were both underweight and would need intensive care. The doctor told me that my sister and the babies needed to stay in the hospital until they were stronger. The hospital allowed family members to visit every day and deliver food if they wished.

I took a bus home and found Mother still asleep. After gathering my overtime working papers together, I went off to work. I told my boss that my sister had just delivered twins, and that she needed help. I asked permission to take off all of the forty days I had accumulated. My boss acquiesced.

My sister stayed in the hospital for a week, as expected. During that week, I visited her every day after work and bought food for her. I was overjoyed to see her and the twins getting stronger every day. I didn't tell her the food I delivered was paid for with my own money, since Mother refused to contribute. After a week, I called a cab to take my sister and the babies to our home.

My mother had not visited my sister once during that week in the hospital. The day before my sister was to come home, Mother told me that because she needed her sleep, she would move to the third floor when the babies arrived home. She would let my sister and I sleep in the second floor bedroom and look after the twins. I didn't mind at all, since I'd already decided to do a proper parent's job in helping my sister.

For the first time in my life, I looked after and slept with a newborn baby. The twins were tiny, and their faces were full of wrinkles. When I touched those tender, soft little hands and feet, they curled into tiny fists. The boys were named Chen Hai and Chen Yong. Chen was the family surname. Hai is *sea* in English, and Yong is *ocean*. Hai and Yong both cried a lot, but one cried louder than the other. I gave Hai the nickname "Tenor" and Yong became "Bass." My sister was sleeping with the tenor, the one with the small head injury that needed more attention, and I had the bass. The first week, I was excited and nervous, fearing that I might fall asleep and miss the feeding every three hours. I constantly checked the time. After a week, I'd become very fatigued. By the second week, I had no problem falling asleep and only woke up when the baby cried. By the third week, even when the baby was crying, I didn't wake up. I needed my sister shaking my shoulder to rouse me. I was just too tired and too young to be a surrogate mother.

I still had to get up early in the morning to buy food at the market, especially for my sister, who needed extra nutrition to help her recover from her recent operation and to nourish her enough to produce milk for the twins. Every night, my mother would give me some money and ration tickets and tell me what to buy for the next day. She gave me so little that it was not enough food for the three of us, and especially not enough to provide proper nutrition for my sister. When I asked Mother for more money, she told me that I should ask my sister for some.

For the first two weeks, I did get some money from my sister, but the third week, she started crying when I asked for more. She told me that on the very first day when she arrived in Shanghai, she had given Mother some money. She had brought more than enough to pay for two month's meals, because she knew she would need some help. She'd been hoping Mother would be reasonably nice to her, and she would make a good recovery from the delivery. Before she'd left home, she and her husband had already borrowed cash from their friends and colleagues.

"Now I don't have any money left," she cried. "Since I don't have enough milk to feed my two babies, after these two months I'm going to have to take one with me back to Guilin and leave the other one with someone who has enough milk to feed him. It will cost a lot to do that. It worries me so much that I can't sleep well, but I would rather suffer myself if it means my sons are well-fed." Then she reached for my hand and said, "Hui Zhi, can you help me to find a suitable wet nurse to feed one of my sons before I return to Guilin?"

"I will," I promised. I held her hand and cried with her.

At the dinner table that night, I screwed up my courage to speak up to Mother. "Sister has already given you enough money to pay for cost of living here for two months. She doesn't have any money left to pay twice for her food. You need to give me more money tonight for tomorrow's food shopping, including Sister's portion."

"What? Give you more money?" Mother replied, very upset. "It's none of your business. I don't need to discuss this with you. Why does she not speak for herself?"

"Have you seen that she isn't eating well, sleeping well, and hasn't recovered well from the operation? The twins are costing her more than she can afford. She is broke already!"

Mother became even more upset at my persistence. "How dare you argue with me!" She stared at me angrily. "You are the worst of all my daughters!"

My sister overheard this and started crying again. "Please don't fight because of me! I will pay more."

This made me even angrier. I no longer cared to bottle up my feelings. "It's not fair to Sister! You are her mother. You shouldn't try to make money off your own daughter when she needs help! I have never seen a mother like you. It's disgusting!" Then I ran out of the house to cool my anger by walking in the darkness.

No one in our family had ever shown enough courage

to argue with Mother. It was my first and last face-to-face argument with her. Although I had been unhappy with her before, I had always kept my feelings inside. This was a big deal for both of us, but I did not win. As usual, my mother triumphed, whether she was right or wrong. My sister asked her husband to borrow more money and wired it to Mother to pay double for her food. During the two months that she stayed in our home, she developed severe sleeping disorders, and later on she found that she had developed liver problems as well.

Much like my mother in our house, Chairman Mao always prevailed in our country, whether wrong or right. Vice chairman Liu Shaoqi had been in detention since 1967 and later died after catching pneumonia. Deng Xiaoping had wisely stepped down after his famous long and deep self-criticism and survived by promising to never try to come to power again. Many potential Capitalists and intellectuals were tortured, and some committed suicide. The whole country was upside-down, and most citizens had lost hope and trust in their government.

Following my forty days of leave, I went back to the factory and decided to eat lunch there from now on. I would finish my meal and lay my head on top of my arms on the table and take a nap. By now I was exhausted and had lost twenty pounds, but I still had to fulfil my promise to find a wet nurse. Through a colleague, I found a mother who had delivered a son three months before and thought that she had enough breast milk to feed two babies. My sister decided to pay the woman a visit, and I came along. She lived in a western suburb of Shanghai, Songjiang. We had to take three different buses and walk part way. It took four hours to finally reach the prospective wet nurse's home.

The woman's last name was Chang, so we called her Chang-Mama. Her home was very dark and small, with only a few simple pieces of furniture sitting on the dirt floor. Her husband, she told us, worked very hard in the fields. Chang-Mama seemed to be an honest and healthy woman, so my sister decided to take the risk and let this woman feed her son for ten months.

Before she returned to Guilin, she took one of her babies to Chang-Mama's home. It was hard to choose which one of her sons to leave behind. In the end she chose to send away Chen Hai, the tenor. The reason was that Chen Hai had already had two months of good care, including the most breastfeeding. She believed Hai was stronger than Yong, who had been cared for by me and fed with milk powder. We went back to Chang-Mama's village, this time taking little Hai with us.

Before we left the village, my sister said to Chang-Mama, "Please take care of my son. If you don't have enough milk to feed two babies, please use the milk powder to feed him. You don't need to worry about the cost; my sister will bring as much as you need."

During the next ten months, I went to visit Hai once a month on Sunday and brought Chang-Mama money and milk powder. I would stay for about two hours, give my little nephew a bath and hold him for a while. If I noticed that Hai had caught a cold or had diarrhoea, I would come back the following Sunday with medicine.

The ten months passed quickly, and my sister again returned to Shanghai, this time to switch the twins. Since Guilin didn't have offer public day-care until children reached two years of age, and my sister couldn't handle both twins and work as an accountant at the same time, she took Hai home with her from Songjiang and brought Yong to stay in Shanghai for a year with his new babysitters, a retired couple who were my neighbours. They didn't have any children of their own and were happy to look after Chen-Yong for a year. They were from Szechuan and couldn't speak the Shanghainese dialect, so we called the husband Szechuan-Yeye and his wife Szechuan-Mama. They were a nice couple and their home was clean. My sister remained in Shanghai for

Chen-Hai and Chen-Yong

a few days to organize the switch then took the train with Hai back to Guilin. She told me that she had difficulty making conversation with Mother, and I realized she had been wounded as badly as I.

My nephew "Bass" was a very handsome boy, with smooth skin and a well-formed nose. He had a wide forehead and large eyes. I visited him almost every day after work to play games, read to him, and teach him songs. Sometimes I pretended to be a horse and let him ride on my back, enjoying his happy laughter. When he was a newborn, I had slept with him, fed him with milk powder and changed his diapers for two months, and now that I saw him and played with him every day, I had started to build a strong bond with him. I believed that I would be a good mother for him. My belief that a mother's job was to give love, protect her children and provide enough food and a safe home. This was the love and protection I had not received.

When a child grows up, a mother should be a friend to that child. She should respect the child's opinions and decisions. I dreamed of adopting this boy, but I knew my sister loved her twins dearly and that she would sacrifice anything for them, so there was no need to ask.

Shortly after my sister's two-month visit, my maternal grandmother moved in with us. I didn't even know how old she was, since my mother's relationship with her was remote. I'd only seen her once a year, at New Year when my mother allowed us to visit our uncle's family. My grandmother had two children, my mother and a son. After her husband passed away, she'd lived with my uncle's family. My uncle was married with three daughters. After my grandmother lived with his family for many years, he thought that it only fair that his sister share in supporting their mother. However, my mother believed that my grandmother was really being kicked out because she was getting too old to assist with the housework.

My grandmother had grown up in the era when Chinese girls' feet were bound. Her two bound feet were about five inches long and three inches thick. Mothers had bound their daughters' feet to make them as small as possible, a demonstration of beauty according to the standards of the time, in hopes that their daughters would marry into a rich family. The process of binding the feet was very painful and cruel. The tight bandages gradually caused the bones of the young girl's feet to break. My grandmother walked very slowly, and when she did, she had to shift her weight from left to right just like a willow tree waving in a changing wind.

My mother told me to move up to the third floor and let Grandmother sleep in the Pagoda Room, in which I had slept for years. This room was the worst in the whole house. The summer was very hot, and the winter was very cold without heat, especially with the cement floor and broken windows. Since Grandmother was in her seventies and couldn't provide any money or labour, she was totally dependent on her daughter. It surprised and distressed me to see that my mother treated her own mother even worse than she treated me. At every meal, she would now sort food into three portions: the best for herself, second-best for me, and the worst for Grandmother. Once Grandmother managed to sneak out of the house and show the neighbours what a tiny serving her daughter had given her. I don't know how my mother found out, but she raged and scolded Grandmother almost every day about small things and complained that Grandmother lived like a lazy pig.

On Sunday, the only day that I had free time to spend at home, I noticed that Grandmother enjoyed sitting alone at the window, watching people on the street. She also talked to herself a lot. When mother was scolding her, she always kept silent. I could picture the weekdays when I wasn't home and how hard it must have been for Grandmother to spend time with her unloving daughter, but I didn't know how to help. All I could do was speaking kindly to her and sometimes share my food with her.

Because winters were so cold in Shanghai, Grandmother eventually caught a chill and fell ill with a high fever. Finally, after she'd lain in bed for a week breathing with difficulty, my mother agreed to call a doctor. I went to the hospital to ask for a house call. My mother let the doctor into Grandmother's room, told me to leave then closed the door. I stayed outside and put my ear to the door to listen. I heard the doctor ask mother some questions about Grandmother's medical history, then I heard the sounds of a physical check-up. After a while, I heard the doctor say, "Your mother has caught a cold and has a fever because this room is too cold, due to its cement floor and broken windows. Normally the antibiotic will kill the infection and bring the temperature down to normal, but since your mother has a chronic infection of her bronchial tubes with asthma, and because she is over seventy, if the fever is not brought down right way, the infection will go to her heart. It will cause her heart to become infected, and she will likely die. I suggest that you take your mother to hospital, where we can use intravenous to bring her temperature down quickly. Also the hospital can handle any complications."

"I understand," Mother said. "Thank you very much, Doctor." I tiptoed downstairs quickly before the door opened. After the doctor left, I waited for my mother to order me to send Grandmother to hospital, but the instruction never came. She didn't even move Grandmother to the second floor, which was the warmest room we had. She did nothing to help her mother, just left her alone in the cold room and waited for her to die. One week later, my grandmother passed away.

I was both angry with my mother, who had shown no compassion towards her own parent and at the same time, felt guilty that I hadn't stood up for Grandmother and tried to save her life. The anger and guilt was to remain inside me for thirty years.

1973–1985

On October 25, 1971, we heard that Vice Chairman Lin Biao had attempted to assassinate Chairman Mao then, having failed, had tried to flee to the Soviet Union. However, his plane crashed in Mongolia. The news was shocking. We were told to remove Lin's portrait from the wall. The man we knew as a hero of the revolution had now become a man despised.

After Lin Biao's death, Mao allowed the Gang of Four—Zhang Chun-Qia, Yao Wen-Yuan, Wang Hong-Wen and Jiang Qing, Mao's second wife—to continue the Cultural Revolution, which was still technically ongoing. When Mao had married Jiang Qing prior to the start of the Cultural Revolution, several high officials had held a meeting to prevent her from any involvement in national politics and Premier Zhou Enlai recorded this in an official document. However, Mao overruled his premier, though the three men in the gang hadn't held high political positions before. The Gang of Four was unpopular in China because they encouraged people to turn on each other. On their orders, a number of high officials were jailed and tortured.

On January 8th, 1976, Premier Zhou Enlai died. During the dark years of the Cultural Revolution, he had been the people's hope for better days. We knew that he tried to make the country work better and had protected a number of people as far as his authority allowed. Most Chinese, including myself, shed genuine tears at the news of his death. Everyone wore a black armband and a white paper flower on their chest. On April 5th, a few months after Zhou's death, came the Tomb-Sweeping Festival, when the Chinese traditionally pay their respects to the dead. In Beijing, hundreds of thousands of citizens gathered in Tiananmen Square to mourn Zhou with specially crafted wreaths, passionate poetry readings, and speeches. The citizens were not only showing their sorrow at Zhou's death but were also subtly demonstrating their anger towards the Gang of Four. The protest was crushed by armed police intervention, and hundreds of people were arrested. Tiananmen Square was awash in blood and the nation fell into deeper shadow.

On July 28th, 1976, Tangshan (a coal-mining city near Beijing) experienced a severe earthquake, an unprecedented disaster that took the lives of 242,000 people injured 164,000 more. Mao refused to allow foreign media to report on the disaster and turned down offers of international aid.

Then, on the September 9th, 1976, came the greatest shock of all—the death of Chairman Mao himself. The whole country watched Mao's funeral ceremony on TV. On cue, we all had to bow our heads three times to show our respect. The new Chairman, Hua Guofeng, delivered the obituary. Hua had been handpicked as Mao's successor. Mao had told Hua, "You are the only person I can trust." Overriding the Chairman's own wishes, the Politburo decided that Mao's embalmed body must be preserved forever in Beijing so that people could visit it and revere him as the greatest Chinese leader in history.

The grief of some of the people mourning for Mao was genuine, but for others, including me, it was just a show. However, the mood of the nation was unmistakably against continuing Mao's policies and especially against the Gang of Four. Less than a month after Mao's death, on October 6th, the Gang of Four was arrested, including Mao's wife. In 1981 the Gang of Four ware subjected to a televised show trial. I watched with keen interest, happy to see that their destructive influence was finally behind us.

In July 1977, Deng Xiaoping was rehabilitated and made

deputy to Hua Guofeng because of his undeniable organizational skills. Deng began a process of change in China. He believed that the Communist party's policies must be based on reality, not dogma. He said, "I don't care if it is a white cat or a black cat, as long as the cat can catch mice, then it is a good cat." In December 1978, the government started to correct some of Mao's leftist polities. They redressed some of the past mistakes such as persecution of "rightists" and former high officials. It gave us hope, but the corruption was severe and the "back door" always opened wider than the "front door." Despite the problems, some effective changes did occur.

In 1974, after I had been working at the carburetor factory for a year, Comrade Wang, our female factory party branch secretary, acknowledged my leadership ability, as well as my dancing and singing talents. At age twenty-three, I became a department manager, and I also took charge of the factory's entertainment team. My salary did not change.

Our factory had ten departments, and each department had two mangers and one quality controller to check the products daily. We had about twenty office workers to lead the factory—such as engineers, accountants and doctors—but none of them had a university degree. They had been appointed by the factory director and the leader of the Communist Party branch secretariat. After their appointment, they had short training sessions with professionals, including doctors (we called the doctor in our factory clinic the "barefoot doctor," since he had only received six months' training). Comrade Wang was the real boss of our factory. She was a very strict and imperious person, and all important decisions were confirmed by her. In China, the Communist Party ruled over all, no matter what their professional qualifications.

Since I was in charge of the factory entertainment team, I selected twelve young girls to learn to dance and sing and six people to play musical instruments. When I taught dance to the girls, the instrumental team refused to provide the music, because the pace was too slow and boring for them. Unfortunately, the factory hadn't provided any recorded music for me to play back. I had to sing the music while I taught dance. Our team received many rewards, but after a year of hard work, I lost my voice. The "barefoot doctor" sent me to hospital to see a real surgeon, and I had a throat operation shortly after that. My voice was supposed to return to normal after three months, but it did not. After six months, the doctor found out that my vocal chords hadn't healed properly, and it was now too late for a second one. Since that time, my voice has been very low-pitched.

By September of 1976, the Cultural Revolution was near its end, and I decided to go to university. I would need the factory director's permission to apply for enrolment, and I would need to pass the entrance exams. In accordance with my ambitions and interests, I would have liked to have become a musician, teacher or doctor, but our factory director, Comrade Gao, refused to give me approval to apply in those areas. "If you want my permission to study at a university, the only area you can study is mechanical engineering, because I can still use you when you graduate." I hated dealing with machines, but I thought that any university education would be better than none at all. I reluctantly agreed to study mechanical engineering and applied to enter the Shanghai University of Industry.

I passed all the entrance exams and began my studies with seven male students from our factory as classmates. Since all high schools and universities had been shut down for ten years during the Cultural Revolution, the first year was devoted to reviewing the high school curriculum. Thereafter, students had to take many more exams and, if they achieved an average of eighty-five per cent or higher, they could on to four years of mechanical engineering courses. My factory agreed that if I worked half days, I could still draw my minimum salary from the factory on the condition that I promised to continue working there after graduation.

I qualified and my next five years as a student-worker was extremely busy. I got up at five in the morning to shop at the food market, then from six-thirty to seven-thirty I practiced tai-chi in the park. From eight to noon I worked at the factory and from one in the afternoon to eight in the evening I studied at the university. From nine to eleven I did my homework. When examination week arrived, I studied through the night. As always, I was a class chairman and a teacher's assistant during my five years at the university.

In the summer of 1981, at the age of thirty, I graduated with a degree in mechanical engineering and returned to work at the factory as a quality control engineer. My salary was raised from thirty-three renminbi to thirty-nine renminbi a month. I was the first female engineer in the factory to obtain a university degree (Six male students from our factory had failed. One male student and I graduated, and both of us became mechanical engineers.) There were three other workers in our quality control office, each responsible for the quality of the three departments that made the components, while I was responsible for the quality of all of the fully assembled carburetors. Before our carburetors were shipped out, it was my job to check their quality and sign for them. It was a heavy responsibility. Though I often found that parts did have quality problems, sometimes it was too late, because the factory had already made thousands of them. No one found out at an early enough stage that an especially negligent colleague had already confirmed that parts met our quality-control standards. I had to make the uncomfortable decision of whether to refuse the parts and overrule my own colleague. I found it frustrating working with people who didn't have the proper training and did not fulfill the responsibilities of their jobs. As a result, jealousy and resentment were my rewards for diligence and integrity.

After a year in my position, I received a troubling letter from one of our important customers, a large motor factory in the city of Chongqing, complaining about the quality of our carburetors. This important customer refused to pay and wanted to return the entire shipment. It would have been a huge financial loss as well and it would have caused severe damage to our reputation. I was very worried, so I checked my records carefully for five per cent of those carburetors that I had tested, and those records showed that they all had met the quality requirements. I showed the test records to the factory director, Gao. They proved that problem was not our fault.

After Gao communicated the findings to the Chongqing Motor Factory, they refused to accept our explanation that tests demonstrated that the goods left our factory in good condition. If they continued to refuse to pay, it would prevent us from buying new material for other orders. There would be insufficient funds to pay salaries. The situation looked dire, so we held an emergency meeting of all of our office staff. The meeting went on for several hours, with no solution being found. It was not my responsibility to solve the factory's financial problems, but I felt that since I worked there, the factory had became my family and that it was my job to help if I could. I offered to visit the Chongqing Motor Factory in person to negotiate and fix the problem and to try my best to convince them to pay us as soon as possible. Actually, I already had a theory about why the carburetors that had worked in Shanghai behaved differently in Chongqing, but I would have to prove it.

In middle of October, I took two workers with me to Chongqing by train. Chongqing is a mountain city located at the northerly bend of the Yangtze River. It is well known for hot, humid summers and cold, foggy winters. When we arrived, I had a meeting with their director and engineers. At the meeting, I showed them the test records and shared my theory that differences in climate, humidity and air pressure between the two cities and the different times of year when the tests had taken place might account for the problems. Working on this hypothesis, we agreed to retest one per cent of all the products in Chongqing.

The October results were much better than the ones from August. Furthermore, if the tester adjusted the ratio of gas to air during the test, the results varied. I was surprised to find out that they had ten people doing the testing, but four were new to the job. Those new workers didn't have enough experience in adjusting for the best ratio of gas to air in the engine. After a week of testing, the Chongqing Motor Factory's managers felt better about our quality and agreed to pay our factory in full. I arranged for two of our workers to stay there and continue making repairs as long as needed, then I returned to Shanghai. I was happy to have fixed the problem, and I felt confident that I had done a good job.

One afternoon shortly after I returned, I went to Director Gao's office to ask some questions. As I stood outside the door preparing to knock, I realized there was a meeting going on. I was about to turn away when I heard my name come up. The voice I recognized as belonging to Party Secretary Wang.

"Comrades, remember Xiao Song comes from a Capitalist family. She may be a good engineer and we can use her—but we can never trust her."

A few days later, I found out that the meeting had been called to nominate someone for a reward from the factory for that year's special contribution, and a few people had recommended me, since I had done such a good job in Chongqing. The nomination was rejected by Party Secretary Wang, and she had been making a speech about it when I'd arrived. I didn't care too much about rewards, but I was hurt that I'd been loyal to our factory and not been trusted as I deserved.

I now realized that, try as I might to change my status from blue collar worker to white collar, I would never be able to change my family's colour from Capitalist black to worker red. It was unfair to judge me based on my father's career, even though he had never hurt anyone and had on the contrary, helped a lot of people. Now I wanted nothing more than to leave this factory. I'd worked hard and shown loyalty, but I knew that I would never be trusted in return.

In 1983, when I was thirty-two, China finally allowed its citizens more freedom, including the right to apply to any university or college without permission, so I enrolled at the Shanghai Traditional Medicine School. I hoped that by taking this course I might leave the factory behind and enter a field better suited to my interests and future happiness.

Since I still had to earn a living, I took an evening course and kept my job at the factory. I was chairperson of my class again, and after two years, I received my diploma in acupuncture and tui na, a Chinese system of massage, acupoint stimulation, and manipulation that's similar to massage and shiatsu. Tui na uses forceful manoeuvres, including pushing, rolling, kneading, rubbing, and grasping, sometimes in conjunction with acupuncture.

5 The Retreat of Love

1979–1984

In China, most girls get married before the age of twenty-five and after that age, family and society apply increasing pressure to marry. In my case, the pressure was applied in the form of gossip. Some people thought I was too picky; some thought I was too old to be attractive.

When I was twenty-seven, a mutual friend introduced me to a young man, Zhang Wei, three years older than me. He'd played cello in the Shanghai Worker's Cultural Palace Symphony, where I too had played until I went to university in 1976. Wei came from an educated family: His father was an engineer and his mother worked in a bank. We often spent time with one of his uncles, who also played, and we talked about our mutual love of classical music. I started dating Zhang Wei and a year later we decided to get married.

Shanghai is a big city. At that time, most families lived in tiny spaces, and some shared one room among three generations. My boyfriend Wei and his parents were such a family, living together in one large room. They'd built a shelf for Wei to sleep on. He had two sisters and a brother; one sister was married and lived in her own place, and the other brother and sister worked in the fields. After China became the People's Republic, the government owned everything, and no private residences were allowed. Then came the Cultural Revolution, and the government placed another family on the first floor in our home. Nonetheless, we continued to occupy a generous space relative to others.

If we got married, we would not be able to live in Wei's family's tiny space. I also knew the government wouldn't rent more space to us, because my family home was too big. Our house was really the only place my husband and I could live in after the marriage, but my mother would have none of it. She accused me of trying to take her property away from her. The truth was she wanted to pass the house on to my brother. I wasn't interested in the ownership of my father's property, which had in fact been left to our whole family, I still needed a place to live.

I spoke to officials at my factory and in the community who were in charge of rental affairs and asked them to rent us a room after we got married. I told them that my mother had refused to let me stay in my own home, and I assumed that she would force me out if we married. In fact, I dearly hoped that she would do just that so I could at last live without her control. The government rental officials didn't like the idea and wanted to talk to my mother themselves. I didn't want them to do that, but I had no choice. My mother and the government continued to control my life.

After two months of negotiation between government officials and my mother, Mother finally agreed to let us live on the third floor. She took pains however to make our lives as difficult as possible. The third floor had a triangular gable roof such that only half of the space was tall enough for an adult to stand up in. I wanted to renovate it so that I could make full use of the space, but my mother refused, and also gave us a list of new house rules:

1. We were forbidden to cook in the kitchen.
2. We were forbidden to use the bathroom inside the house.
3. We were forbidden to eat in the normal dining place on the first floor.
4. We were only allowed to buy two bamboo poles to hang our laundry, and they had to be hung at the top of the third floor stairs.
5. I had to clean the whole house, including Mother's part, and do her laundry once a week.

Zhang Wei and I were married on October 1st, 1979. Three of my sisters and my brother attended the wedding. When they arrived, my mother asked my brother to put three bulky suitcases on the third floor outside my bedroom door. Not only did it look unsightly, but navigating around them was highly inconvenient. Two of my sisters stayed with relatives, but my second sister Hui Li and her daughter needed to stay at our place. My mother told them to sleep on the floor in my room. When Hui Li told me this news, I was very upset. We would have no privacy on our wedding night and honeymoon. There was nothing I could do. While I was helping my sister and her daughter set up their beds on the floor in my room, my eldest sister, Hui Ling, came to visit.

"Why doesn't Hui Li sleep in Pagoda Room?" she wondered. "It's empty."

"Mother told me to sleep in Hui Zhi's room," Hui Li explained.

Hui Ling frowned. "Hui Li, you can sleep in the available room if you choose, especially on Hui Zhi's honeymoon.

Doesn't that make sense?"

Hui Li moved out of my room. Mother nonetheless forbade her to use the empty Pagoda Room and ordered her and her daughter to sleep on the floor in Mother's own bedroom instead. But thanks to the timely support of Hui Ling, Zhang Wei and I had some privacy on our wedding night after all.

After the wedding, I used the small space between the second and third floor stairs for cooking. It was so small that there was only enough space for a Chinese-style stove and no space for a table. I prepared each meal inside the room then brought it out onto the landing to cook it. I had to put all the dishes on the floor beside the stove while I was cooking. The whole process was difficult and dirty and I often tripped over the dishes and spilled the food.

Sanitation was also a problem. Our house had two bathrooms, one on the first floor with only a toilet, the other a three-piece bathroom on the second floor. When I was a child, I was allowed to use any bathroom I wanted, but during the Cultural Revolution, after the government let another family move onto our first floor, I could only use the bathroom on the second floor. After our marriage, we were denied use of either of the washrooms. We couldn't bathe at home any more, which made the hot and humid summers especially difficult. We had to use a chamber pot and keep it inside the room all day. Most of Shanghai's population didn't have flush toilets. In some areas people used a wooden container and put it out in the morning, when the city would collect the waste. But we lived in an area that had a modern sewage system, so we received no service from the city. Every day when I got home from the university, I had to take our chamber pot to the local public bathroom, dump it then walk back home to clean it up. The public bathroom was located just across from the telephone service station. It was especially nasty walking in the cold, dark winter nights carrying this heavy, smelly stuff.

Winters presented further difficulties. All the food had to be washed, and in the morning both of us had to brush our teeth and wash our faces on the open balcony, the cold wind in our faces.

None of this could stop me from loving my husband and enjoying my new life. I had a new blanket, and my husband let me warm my cold feet against his in the winter. We used a coffee table as a dinner table and sat on the couch to eat. It was a wonderful change that we were always willing to give each other the better part of the food. My husband worked a two-shift schedule from six in the morning to two thirty in the afternoon one week, and from two thirty in the afternoon to eleven at night the next week. When he worked the afternoon schedule, I took a break from my morning tai-chi and we walked to the food market together. When he worked the morning schedule, he often followed my notes on cooking. Because I had to work and study every day, we didn't have as much time together as we would have liked. We communicated through delightful little notes.

I was born in the year of rabbit and Wei in the year of the rat. When I left a note for him, I never signed my name, instead drawing a rabbit. Depending on the nature of the message and my mood, I would draw different sorts of rabbits. Wei tried to draw on the notes he left for me too, but he couldn't draw well and most of his results were comical. On Sunday I could be lazy and stay late in bed listening to classical music or perhaps I'd get up and practice the cello. Once a month, Wei and I visited my in-laws for dinner. I laughed often and loudly. For me, life was good.

1979. I am 28
Zhang Wei and I are newly married.
It's he who takes this photo of me and my beloved cello.

Shortly after our third month of marriage, I received a letter from my brother. He accused me of being a selfish sister who had badly mistreated our mother. He complained that during my honeymoon I had refused to share my room with Hui Li and had forced her to sleep in Mother's room.

My selfish behaviour had been demonstrated further after my marriage, because I had cut off my relationships with my siblings. As further evidence of my selfishness, he pointed out that I laughed loudly with my husband but never shared the jokes with our mother.

I didn't consider arguing with him. I knew that my mother was behind all of this, trying to make me feel uncomfortable and inconvenient, hoping I would one day leave her house. I'd got that message long before I was married, but to her frustration and surprise, I showed a lot of joy in my new life. Since the government controlled Shanghai's housing policy so tightly, I had no idea if I'd ever be able to move out.

In the spring of 1980 came the stunning news that the government had decided to allow citizens to visit relatives who lived abroad. There were strict rules, but at least China had opened its door a crack to the world. Some credit was no doubt due to Richard Nixon. This small liberalization was soon to have a huge and unexpected effect on my life.

My father-in-law had been born and educated in Thailand. After graduating from university, he'd decided to live in China. He'd worked and built a family in China and until now hadn't been able to visit his relatives in Thailand. He qualified to go to Thailand for a visit under the government's new policy. He had an eyesight problem—his range of vision was narrower than normal—and this provided compassionate grounds for and the visit. He could take one family member with him and that person would be my husband, Wei.

After the Cultural Revolution, many Chinese citizens had lost all faith in the government. They wanted desperately to get out of China and had very naïve and false ideas about conditions in other countries, especially the United States. At that time, most people thought that as soon as anyone landed in America, he or she would get rich right away. They thought that people could pick up gold in the streets.

Because I was studying at university and was also a chairperson of our class, I had opportunities to read the "Small Newspaper." This paper was called "small" not only because it was physically smaller than the regular newspapers, but also because its circle of readers was smaller. It reported world news that only a few were allowed to read. I had some knowledge of Thailand already at that time. I understood that it was a male-dominated country and that its economy wasn't any better than China's. Nonetheless, I supported my husband's decision to go with his father. This was the only chance I might have to move out of our home and I hoped that Wei would stay in Thailand and sponsor my entry into that country.

At the end of the summer of 1980, after nearly a year of marriage, Wei went with his father to Thailand for the three-month visit. They took the train from Shanghai to Guangzhou to get to Hong Kong. From Hong Kong they flew to Bangkok. I was in tears when I bade Wei farewell at the train station. It was difficult for me to let him go and I missed him very much.

After about three weeks, I received his first letter. He told me about their safe arrival and his basic impressions of Bangkok. For the next two months, the letters concerned how he could legally stay in Thailand. He told me about the country's immigration laws and how his relatives were trying to help them stay there. In the end, he told me that they'd tried every avenue to get the immigration done legally, but the Thai government did not welcome people from mainland China. The only way for him to stay was to claim refugee status, but he would have to destroy his Chinese passport to hide his identity, and hopefully one day the Thai government would allow an amnesty. If he used this plan, he would have to wait at least five years without any guarantee of success.

The sad news for me was that I would not be able to be with him for that long period. It troubled me that he would take such a big risk without any guarantee of success, leaving me in limbo in China. After careful thought, I replied to his letter, asking him to return home. I wrote,

> My darling, five years is too long for me to live without you. We are a married couple, and therefore I believe we should share our lives, whether we are rich or poor. I believe that as long as we love each other, we will find a way to live freely and better… I miss you so much and find it so hard to wait to be with you again.
>
> Lots of love and XOXO.

In his next letter he said that he agreed with me and that he would return home soon. In the meantime, he'd extended his visitor's visa another three months and, in order to earn enough money to buy a TV and refrigerator to bring home, he'd started working illegally for cash through a relative's connection at a factory. I appreciated his effort.

That was the last letter I received from him. No matter how many I wrote, he just seemed to have disappeared. It worried me so much that I couldn't eat or sleep well. I phoned my mother-in-law many times to ask her for news. She said that she hadn't received any letters from her husband either. I decided to mail Wei a tape recording of me playing a piece on the cello that both of us loved deeply. Since I didn't have a tape recorder, I asked my mother-in-law it I could borrow one. She said that she didn't have one either, but she would ask her son-in-law to lend me his.

I went to my mother-in-law's home to pick up the tape recorder arriving a little earlier than she had requested. I found her sitting at the table, reading a letter. I was immediately cheered and hopeful. I said good afternoon to her. "Is that a letter from Dad you're reading?"

"No," she answered. She put the letter into a pocket and we chatted for a half hour.

"I've bought a movie ticket and I have to go now," she finally said. "You can wait here for my son-in-law to bring the recording machine. He was supposed be here an hour ago." She glanced at her watch. "I guess he may be stuck in the traffic, but he should arrive shortly."

After she left, I waited for a while, but my brother-in-law didn't show up. The image of my mother-in-law reading the letter had raised a question in my mind. Could she be hiding something from me? I started looking around, and to my surprise, I found five letters from my father-in-law, all dated during the previous three months. When I read them, I was shocked. He told my mother-in-law that in the beginning Wei had been very active in trying to find a way to immigrate to Thailand, but lately he had changed his mind and just wanted to make some extra money, then return home. His father and relatives suspected that his wife had influenced him to come home, when the family wanted to move to Thailand.

Since Wei worked during the day, his family had decided to open my letters to him whenever a letter arrived from me. Reading them confirmed their suspicion that I was influencing him to change his mind. My wishes were opposed to my in-laws' wishes. They hoped that Wei would stay in Thailand and sponsor his siblings. They believed that he was the only hope for their family in getting the family out of China.

Because I wanted my husband to return home, they hated me. In my father-in-law's letter, he referred to me as the "devil" that would bring bad luck to them. After reading my letters, he'd thrown them in the garbage and made up a story to tell Wei. He'd told his son that he'd received the news from his mother that I had a new boyfriend and that I had a bad reputation in Shanghai. He told Wei that I had totally forgotten him and he advised Wei to date other girls. Through their relatives, they'd introduced him to Chinese-Thai women, and my father in-law wrote that he was glad to see Wei forget me so quickly. He hoped his son would marry a local woman and thus get his Thai citizenship.

My hair stood up over my entire body and I couldn't think or feel anything clearly. Somehow I got back to my own home. I cried through the night until morning. The next day I noticed a tuft of white hair on top of my head. I was twenty-nine.

I didn't record the cello music or write any more letters. It was useless, since my mail would not get through to him, but I didn't believe that he had forgotten me that quickly. I needed to come up with a way let him know the truth. I decided to call him, though I didn't have a phone number. It took three months but I finally got Wei's relatives' telephone number through a friend's relative who lived in Bangkok.

I couldn't make long distance calls from our local telephone station. There was only one international telephone station in Shanghai. On a Saturday evening, I went to the station. It was very busy and I had to join a line. The station operators would dial the number for me while I waited in a small room. If I saw my telephone room's light start flashing, I should pick up the phone.

The light flashed. I picked up the phone and heard Wei's voice. I had so many things to tell Wei, but I began to cry instead and cried for five minutes

"Is anyone sick or dying?" Wei asked. "Why have you made an emergency long distance call?"

"No one's sick," I said. "I just miss you and want to talk to you."

Wei told me his father and relatives were listening to the conversation. He wanted me to write to him instead.

"No, Wei. Wait, please! I want you to know that your father has behaved very badly by opening my letters. He's read them and thrown them out when you weren't home. Your parents are planning to rid themselves of me because I want you to come home!"

"That's nonsense!" His voice was cold and remote. "I don't believe it. They're good to me. I must go. I'll write to you. Bye." The phone went dead. The call had cost me a month's salary.

I didn't know what to do. I needed help. My mother didn't offer any, nor did she ask me any questions when she heard me crying almost every night. Ten years before, I'd asked her to help me break up with Fa Ling, and the coldness of her answer still chilled me. I feared asking for her help again. Instead I talked to two girlfriends at our factory. One of them advised me to move into my mother-in-law's home. "Tell your mother-in-law that you want your husband back, or you will stay there as long as Wei remains in Thailand. You must report the truth to your mother-in-law's local community officers and ask them to pressure her to help with your husband's return."

I listened to her advice and moved into my mother-in-law's home and reported her to the local community officer. She hated me for this. Now I realized she was the one who'd advised my father-in-law to make up the story to damage my reputation and distance Wei from me. It was difficult living with someone I disliked so and after three tense days, I moved back into my own house again. I wrote a letter to the Chinese embassy in Thailand asking them to help me to get Wei to return. I never received any answer from them.

Another three months passed, but it seemed like a lifetime to me. It was difficult getting through each day without news. One night, about a year after Wei had left for Thailand, our neighbour, Aunt Ma, who lived on the first floor, shouted up to me. "Hui Zhi, you have a visitor!" I was doing my homework on the third floor. I dropped my pen and ran down to the front door. To my astonishment, I saw Wei standing outside. My first reaction was to jump towards him and give him a hug, but there was no sign of warmth from him.

I closed the front door and said, "Let's go to our room."

When he sat down, I looked at him intently. After being away for a year, he looked darker and slimmer and had started to grow a beard. He seemed uncomfortable.

"Why didn't you let me know you were coming? If I'd known, I'd have been happy to have met you at the train station."

"We flew to Shanghai this time," he answered.

"When?" I asked.

"Two days ago," he said.

"What? Two days ago?" I sat down suddenly on the sofa. Now I knew something was really wrong. I hadn't been informed of his return and he'd been in Shanghai two days. I looked at him again. He didn't have any luggage and held only a small plastic bag.

"Oh, I brought some dresses for you." He handed me the bag. It contained a few second hand polyester dresses.

"Where are the TV and fridge?" I asked.

"At my parents' house. They belong to my father." He looked down at the floor for a few moments, scratched his head then said hesitantly and softly, "Hui Zhi, I wonder if you could agree that…that we can get a divorce."

"Go to hell!" I shouted. "You want a divorce so that you can marry a woman in Thailand, and then your whole family can move there. What a wonderful plan! No, I'm telling you that I will not give you the divorce papers, and you will never go back there!" I was enraged. "Out! Get out of here! I never want to see you again!"

How could he have changed so quickly? What had I done to deserve so unkind a fate? My happiness had vanished.

The following week, Wei returned to again ask for my agreement to divorce. I refused to speak to him. On Sunday, the day I was supposed to clean the whole house, I forgot to clean the little Pagoda Room, I was so stressed. That night, just before I went to bed, I remembered. I went down, opened the Pagoda Room's door and turned the light on. A face with a dark beard peered at me through the window. I screamed and ran to my bedroom. Clearly Wei's parents' story about me having a boyfriend had poisoned his mind. He had climbed the wall to check on me.

A man called Xiao Chen had worked at the factory and been best friends with Wei before he went to Thailand. During our first year of marriage, we'd invited him over many times. Xiao Chen was a short but strong man. He had a good heart and was honest and sincere. I liked him a lot. Before Wei went to Thailand, he'd asked Xiao Chen to visit me from time to time to see if I needed any help. Xiao Chen had visited me often, especially when I hadn't received any news from Wei. He'd been kind when my in-laws had planned to get rid of me. He believed that the Wei's parents' behaviour towards me had been awful, and he showed me a great deal sympathy. When Wei returned from Thailand, Xiao Chen was not only supportive of me but also critical of his friend, who had become an irresponsible and unfaithful husband. I heard that they'd had a serious fight at their factory, and that Wei had called Xiao Chen a thief who had stolen his wife. But Xiao Chen hadn't bothered to explain the truth, he'd just laughed. After that incident, Xiao Chen visited me one more time to say goodbye. He explained that because Wei suspected he was my boyfriend and was using that to justify divorce, he couldn't stay in touch with me any more. I was thankful to him, and to this day I still regret that I lost touch with him.

Two months passed. It was the end of 1981 and I was thirty when I received a letter from the court stating that Wei had filed for divorce. At that time, divorce was still an unpopular and shameful thing in China. Unless both spouses agreed to it, it required proof of serious misconduct by one spouse.

I had never been to court in my life. To my mind, going to court was serious business. I assumed all judges would handle their cases with fairness. In the middle of December on a Friday afternoon, I attended my first session at the local county court. In the court, the judge announced that my husband Zhang Wei had filed for divorce. Then he asked Wei to provide the reason why he wanted to proceed. Wei said that our marriage was not based on love and that he was an Eastern-type man married to an affectionate Western-type woman who liked to kiss and hug a lot. Of course it was true that I was affectionate. We'd married because of the love we felt for one other. Almost everyone would agree that kissing and hugging expressed loving feelings, even for Eastern couples.

I told the judge that the real reason he wanted the divorce was simply because I'd wanted him to come back to China, but that had conflicted with his parents' wishes. His family wanted him to divorce me first, then marry a Thai woman.

But the judge wouldn't let me finish my explanation. "Zhang Wei is in China now," he said. "My court does not need to talk about Thailand. If you don't want to divorce, it's very simple."

He turned to Wei. "Your wife doesn't want a divorce. You must go and sleep together tonight." Then he laughed. "This court is dismissed," he said.

I was shocked at such cavalier and insulting behaviour. I said nothing more and returned home alone. Wei went his parents' place.

During the second session, the judge pushed me to make a quick decision: agree to divorce or return home and sleep with Wei. He wouldn't let me present any of the significant events that had damaged the marriage. I wondered why he would not handle the case fairly. It seemed that he was determined to take Wei's side and had no interest in hearing my side

"If you will put a clause into the divorce papers that forbids Wei to go to Thailand after the divorce, I'll agree to divorce him now. Otherwise I won't agree to a divorce, and he can't go back to Thailand." The judge refused, so the second session ended without progress.

I was extremely angry. I told myself, "Hui Zhi, wake up. It's time to fight for your basic rights. Do you want to continue living this miserable and totally unfair life?" I decided to fight back, no matter how powerful the judge was and how difficult it would be. I bought a small tape recorder and a bottle of rat poison. I planned to bring them to the next court session. If the judge wouldn't let me tell my side of the story, I would record what he said in the court. If he pushed me to agree to divorce without any discussion of right or wrong, I would drink the bottle of poison and die in front of him. I had lost the most important thing in my life, my husband's love. I wasn't afraid to die if it would make the judge and court show more fairness towards other women. On the other hand, if I could get public support through the media, I would have a better chance of having my voice heard in the court. I followed my dear father's philosophy: try your best and prepare for the worst.

I wrote a ten-page letter describing my marriage and what had happened when Wei was in Thailand, how I'd found out his parents had done such terrible things, and why he had returned to China to ask for a divorce. I also included my opinions about the judge's unfair behaviour. I began looking for a newspaper or magazine that would publish my story. I wanted the public to know the truth so that others would not have to suffer such a fate.

My uncle was an editor with a newspaper called *Wen-Hui-Bao,* the *Cultural Report News.* When I visited him, he told me that he was only the editor of articles about chess. If I wanted to get my letter published, he would have to ask the correct news department. I waited a week then paid him another visit but found out that he hadn't asked anyone yet. He said that he was just too busy, but I knew that he really didn't want to help me.

I moved on to the *Ren-Min-Ri-Bao*—the *People's Daily News*—and to *Xin-Min-Wan-Bao*—the *New People's Evening News Daily*—but again I was unsuccessful. I told myself that I was never to give up. I missed many afternoon classes at the university that some of the students and teachers suggested that I stop studying for a year to concentrate on the divorce case. It would make things easier for me, but I decided to persist and continue my studies as far as possible.

I finally went to a monthly magazine called *Nian-Qing-Yi-Dai*—*Youth Generation*—and asked to talk to an editor or manager. After about fifteen minutes, a tall young woman came out. She introduced herself as Yang Hong, a manager and an editor, and she invited me into her office. She listened patiently as I told my story. Her compassion and sympathy really warmed my heart, and I started to cry. After she finished reading my long letter, she suggested that I remove my complaint about the judge's unfairness. She explained to me that, even though it might all be true, and assuming the judge was taking bribes, he nonetheless represented the government in court. It would be as hard to take on government officials, as it would be for an egg to fight a stone. The chance of success would be low and it could cause me a lot of trouble later on. If I accepted her advice to remove that part of my story and also to cut it from ten pages down to three, she would publish it in the magazine, but the process would take six months. In the meantime, she suggested that I hire a lawyer. That way, the judge would not be able to push me into divorce without my side of story being told. It would also help me avoid dealing with the judge directly, and I could concentrate on my studies.

This thoughtful woman had given me hope. I paid her a second visit after I had reduced my story to three pages. Yong Hong liked my second version, and she told me that she had already contacted the judge who had dealt with my case. She believed it would help me get fair treatment from the court in the future. She told me that the magazine had decided to publish my story not only to support me but also to expose it as a recurring issue in China. With more people leaving the country, there would be more broken marriages, and it could become a big social problem. She hoped that my story would make the government pay attention.

This issue did in fact become a problem. I heard about

temporary laws being instituted such that, if one spouse left China and wanted a divorce, he or she would have to pay twenty thousand U.S. dollars to the spouse who still lived in China. Twenty thousand dollars was the equivalent of twenty year's salary for the average person in China.

I used "Genuine" for my pen name. After my story was published in *Youth Generation* magazine, I received over five hundred responses through the magazine's mailbox. People showed a great deal of sympathy and support. Some men even asked if I would be interested in a date. It touched me deeply, and I took a lot of positive energy from it, but I didn't want to date any more. I'd lost my trust in men.

Yong Hong mailed a copy of the magazine with my story in it to the judge and he totally changed his attitude. He allowed me to speak in court about the terrible wrongs that had been done to me, and he changed his tone from demanding and harsh to soft and friendly. I felt much better, but I still was resistant to the divorce that would allow Wei to marry a Thai woman. At that time, a divorce had to be agreed upon by both sides. My original plan was to never agree to it so that Wei would never have another chance to leave.

I opened the door one morning and there was Wei

"May I talk with you?" he asked.

We were both of us quite tense. Eventually, however, he apologized for thinking that I'd had an affair with Xiao Chen. He admitted climbing the wall to check on me. He said that he now knew all the gossip was wrong.

I started to soften and talked to him from my heart. I told him how much I'd loved him and how much difficulty I'd had the year he was in Thailand.

"I know you have been a good wife to me," he said. "But since my parents are involved, I don't know what to do. They want me to divorce you and marry a Thai woman. My mother cries every day. She asked me to imagine how much effort, love and money she had put into raising me from a little infant only ten inches long to the six-foot-tall man I am today. My father is also upset. Every time he talks to me, it's in an angry voice, pounding on the table. He said that he prefers to die if I won't divorce you. My father has high blood pressure and when he's angry, his face turns bright red. I'm worried that he really will die from a stroke." He started to cry. "I just don't know what to do, Hui Zhi. I still love you."

As soon as I heard the words "I still love you" tears started to flow.

Wei looked up. "Maybe we can get a divorce first," he said. "I could marry a Thai woman to get immigration. After I get status there, I could divorce again and remarry you and bring you to Bangkok."

"No, Wei," I said firmly. "You can't exploit another woman's feelings for you as your family's immigration tool. As soon as you married me, it was your responsibility to love and protect me. If you are going to marry a Thai woman, I want you to love and protect her too. I don't want anyone to suffer what I have suffered. If you don't love her, then don't marry her. If you want to marry her, then do a husband's job and support her!"

I decided to agree to the divorce, since the battle had already been going on for over two years, and I was thirty-two. I told myself that revenge is never for the best. It was time to let Wei go. I didn't even take financial compensation, although I knew the colour TV and refrigerator were mine by right. I didn't want to fight about material things. I'd lost my love and my happy marriage and knew that possessions wouldn't compensate me. I cut off all communication with Wei after the divorce and closed the book on my marriage.

In 1983, the government announced a new regulation that allowed one child to return to Shanghai to live with their parents if the family didn't already have another child living with them. My mother naturally wanted my brother to return to Shanghai, but I occupied the space he could have lived in, so he couldn't come back. My mother badly wanted me to leave and I didn't mind the thought of leaving Shanghai at all. Since my divorce, I'd been badly in need of a change.

That same year, Deng Xiaoping decided to develop business in Shenzhen, a city in Guangdong province across from Hong Kong, without the usual strict government control. I'd heard that Shenzhen needed professionals to build this new economy and with my engineering degree, I hoped to work there. I contacted them for a job interview, but did not have enough engineering work experience. My disappoint was crushing. If I hadn't continued to indulge my passion for the study of traditional Chinese medicine, all purpose would have gone from my life. I had no way of knowing the role Chinese medicine was to play in my future.

BOOK II

6 A Precarious Passage

1985

In 1985, when I was thirty-four, I made a sudden decision. I contacted a distant relative—I called her Aunty Lui—a senior citizen living in Toronto. Aunty Lui agreed to write a letter asking me to visit her in Canada, even though she knew that I intended to stay permanently. In her letter, she informed me that the invitation was to give me a chance to leave China, but she wouldn't provide for me during the time I was "visiting" her. My sister Hui Ling worried that I would have a nervous breakdown if I went to this remote country alone and without help, but at this point I was ready to do anything to change my life. If I were meant to die young, I would prefer it to happen in a foreign country where no one knew me and no one would remember me. I was dead in my heart as long as I lived in this house and in this country. Canada was my last chance to change my fate.

I received the expected invitation letter from Aunty Lui early in 1985. After that, I would need to apply at the police station for a Chinese passport. I knew that in getting a passport, the most important person would be our factory's party branch secretary, who had to agree to let me go. Luckily, the old party branch secretary, harsh Comrade Wong, had recently retired, and her replacement was a Comrade Shi. He was a straightforward man who understood how stressful the divorce case had been for me. I talked to him privately, and he agreed to let me go. He also promised to keep my plans secret. His cooperation came as a big relief, since I'd been worried that he could use any excuse to obstruct me, such as the importance of my job to the factory. He could even have accused me of wanting to go to a Western country to chase the Capitalist life, since it was well known that I had been born into a Capitalist family. The passport application process turned out to be quite easy. The police checked whether I had a criminal record, which of course I did not. After waiting for three months, I received my first passport.

Obtaining a Canadian visa would be most difficult part, but I did get some good advice and coaching from friends. I had practiced tai-chi in the park since I was seventeen and I'd associated with many professionals in the group—doctors, lawyers, and teachers. Some of them had family members living overseas, but I learned that even for those people it had been exceptionally difficult to get a visa. One of my friends, who had parents living in the U.S., told me that he had applied ten times to visit his parents, but his visa application had never been approved. Another member's father was living in France, but the French government had never allowed him to visit his father.

Since I was now single, it would be even more difficult to get a visitor's visa. Some people told me that I would have no chance of getting one from the Canadian embassy. It was discouraging, but I was determined to push on and try my best.

Chapter Six

I went through a Chinese travel agency to organize my interview with the Canadian embassy. A staffer would fly in from Beijing to interview about twenty applicants in an old office building in central Shanghai. I needed to prepare good answers to any questions I might be asked in the interview and my tai-chi group helped me a lot.

The day when it arrived was a sunny and bright. Perhaps good luck, like the sun, would shine on me.

I was the first to be interviewed, shortly after nine A.M. I walked nervously into the room and found myself face to face with a beautiful Canadian immigration officer named Susan. To my amazement, she spoke perfect Mandarin. Before she could ask me any questions, I volunteered that my Aunty Lui was old and ill and wanted me to visit her. I showed her my engineering degree and a copy of my job title from my factory to prove that I had important responsibilities in Shanghai that allowed me to be absent for no more than two months. When the officer asked about my marriage situation, I said that I was divorced, but I also lied and said that I was engaged to a fiancé named Ling Kai, and that we planned to be married on the Chinese New Year that year. I showed her an engagement ring and an engagement photo. She studies my documents and asked me a number of questions.

Finally she looked up.

"I'm going to award you a three month visitor's visa to Canada," she said simply.

I was astonished. She told me that I would need to pass a medical exam, and after she received my medical report, she would mail my passport to me through the travel agency within three months, with a Canadian visitor's visa stamp in it. I was so excited, I wanted to scream or jump up and give this Susan a big hug. Of course, I did not. I kept quiet and cool and walked slowly from the office.

When I was outside, I pedalled as fast as I could to the ferry to Pudong. I ran into an empty field and started to scream, but my cheering soon changed to tears. I looked up at the sky and asked God why I'd been so lucky this time. I'd never had any good fortune in my life. Was this finally the time for me to change my life?

The next morning, when I went to the park for tai-chi, I told everyone the good news and thanked Ling Kai for renting a ring and allowing me to take a photo with him. His support had been critical to my visa application. I thought that everyone was happy for me and wished me a good future in Canada. They all knew my true intent, which was to a new and better life there. Little did I foresee the consequences of my enthusiasm.

I started to prepare for my Canadian journey. I didn't know what to expect of this mysterious country, but I knew I'd need to be healthy to face the difficulties of adapting to a foreign lifestyle. I would face a totally different culture and language and an uncertain future.

I had a cyst on the right side of my lower back. It caused me discomfort from time to time. I asked a friend from tai-chi, who was a surgeon, for an operation to remove it. I took a half day off work and cycled to the hospital. I was relaxed, because I had full confidence in Dr. Pam.

I lay face downwards on the operating table, and Dr. Pam gave me a freezing injection, then he began the operation. At first I only felt a little discomfort, but as soon as he cut deeper to take out the cyst, I felt the shock of a sharp pain. My heart began to race very fast, and I began to vomit. The worried nurse told Dr. Pam that my face had turned pale and that she was afraid that I would faint at any moment. Dr. Pam told me to try breathing slowly, and he would sew me back up as fast as possible with completing the procedure.

"No!" I said. "Inject some more anaesthetic into my back and take out the cyst!"

"Can you handle it?" he asked.

"Yes," I insisted. "Please finish the job!"

Dr. Pam injected more anaesthetic and everything went fine.

"How do you plan to get back home?" he asked. "Is a family member with you?"

"No, there is no one with me. I came by bicycle," I said.

"Are you crazy?" He almost laughed. "Riding a bicycle home after back surgery? Can you call and ask your mother to come here so she can take you home in a taxi?"

"No, my mother is out of town," I lied.

Dr. Pam shook his head and mumbled something before leaving the operation room. A half hour later, he came back with another man whom he said was a truck driver. He had asked the trucker to put my bicycle on the back of the truck. He held my arm as I slowly got into the front seat. The driver took me home and unloaded my bicycle for me then I slowly walked up the stairs to my room. As I passed my mother's room, I kept silent.

On August 23rd, at ten thirty in the morning, I had taken the day off to prepare for my first overseas trip when I received a call from the travel company asking me to go their office as soon as possible. I put some money in my pocket and went on my bicycle, arriving there at around eleven. I guessed that the agent had received my passport from the Canadian embassy in Beijing and wanted me to pick it up. When I arrived, the agent, Lao Ho, rushed out of his office and stopped me in the hallway. He looked around with a strange expression then walked towards the corner opposite his office and asked me to sit on the bench.

"Before I tell you the news, I need you to promise me that you will not cry and that you'll listen to me carefully," he said.

"Okay, I promise."

"Do you have an enemy or someone who is jealous of you for going overseas?"

"I don't know. My tai-chi group knows all of the details of my plan, but they're always kind to me."

"Your passport arrived yesterday afternoon from Beijing," he said. "But I didn't have a chance to give it to you. Last night the Canadian embassy called our office and asked that we withhold it, if you hadn't already received it. They received a letter from Shanghai. Someone who knows you told the Canadian embassy that as soon as you enter Canadian territory, you plan to stay there with no intention to leave. The embassy didn't like that. They'll stop you from entering into Canada and have decided to review your case again."

Lao Ho stopped talking and looked at me worriedly. I believe that my face had turned pale. I felt dizzy but I held back my tears. Lao Ho dropped his voice.

"The good news," he said, "is that last night I wasn't in the office and my colleague Xiao Hua answered the phone. She didn't know where the passport was being kept. It might still have been in the office but also might be in your hands already. She told the Canadian officer that she would pass the message on to me today." He cleared his throat. "Now, listen to me very carefully, Xiao Song. I've decided to give you the passport, but you must try to leave China as quickly as possible. I can't guarantee that you will successfully get into Canada when your plane arrives, but the only thing left for you is to try. If you do get into Canada, my suggestion to you is that you try to socialize with some Chinese students who are studying at universities, because those students may be able to help you." He handed me the passport. "I wish you good luck," he said. "Now run."

I will be forever grateful to Lao Ho. His kindness gave me a chance at freedom.

After the shock of this news, I needed to rethink my plan, but didn't have much time left. I left the building quickly and sat down on the back steps for a few minutes to think.

First, I went to the overseas office in eastern Shanghai to get a paper that permitted me to buy a one-way air ticket to Canada. Then I went to another office in the same area to get some foreign currency. At that time, the government only allowed travellers with a visitor's visa to exchange renminbi for sixty U.S. dollars. By this time, it was already three in the afternoon. I pedalled as hard as possible to get to the international air ticket office in the west end of the city.

When I got there, after waiting in a short line-up, I showed my passport and ticket purchase permission and asked for a one-way ticket to Toronto, if I could leave the next day. "The tickets from Shanghai to Toronto are all sold out," the young sales agent said. "It's high season now, and most people booked the ticket from two to five months in advance. You have to wait about a month and a half to get a flight to Toronto."

"Is there any way I can leave tomorrow?" I asked. "It's an emergency."

"The only ticket left is first class. It costs five thousand renminbi, which is triple the price of an economy class fare. The plane leaves Shanghai at eight o'clock tomorrow morning for Tokyo, then continues on from Tokyo to Vancouver, and from Vancouver to Toronto."

"I'll take it," I said. After the young salesman put all the information into the computer and wrote the ticket for me, he asked for five thousand renminbi in cash. At that time credit cards were not used in China. Everything was paid for in cash. After working for twelve years, I had only saved two thousand renminbi, and most of my savings had already been spent buying gifts for Aunty Lui. After getting American money, I only had ten renminbi left in my pocket. I told the young salesman to hold the ticket for me. I would go to the bank for the money then return.

It was now four thirty, and most banks would be closed at five. There was no time for me to get home even if I had the money, and where could I get the money? I decided to ask my tai-chi teacher, Lou Hong. He was a well-known instructor of tai-chi and qi-gong, but famous for his calligraphy. He had published several books on the history of calligraphy and made money from the sales. He was also well known in Japan. In the past I had seen many Japanese people visiting him. When they met Teacher Lou, they would kneel down in front of him to show their respect. Because of my aptitude for tai-chi, I was one of his favourite students and I had twenty beginner-level students of my own. I knew Teacher Lou had over ten thousand renminbi in savings, and his house was just five minutes away by bicycle from the international ticket office.

I arrived at his door, breathing hard.

"Teacher Lou, can you lend me five thousand renmibi? It's an emergency. I need to pick up my plane ticket before the office closes in twenty minutes."

"What?" Teacher Lou stepped back a little. "What's happened?"

"It's a long story, and I don't have time to explain to you.

The bank will close at five. Could you go to get the cash first?"

"Okay, Hui Zhi." He looked at me. "But I would only do this for you."

He put his bankbook in his pocket and I followed him to the bank. We arrived just before five. I wept with relief.

Suddenly Teacher Lou changed his mind. "Wait a minute," he said. He pulled the money back. "Can you tell me why you have to leave China in such a hurry?"

"Someone from our tai-chi group has betrayed me and written a letter to the Canadian embassy telling them that I am intending to stay in Canada. The embassy wants to take back my visa. That's why I have to go in such a hurry."

"Then why is the visa still in your hands?"

"Because the agent gave it to me just today," I said.

"Who?" Teacher Lou asked.

"I'm sorry, I can't tell you. It's not fair to expose someone who took a big risk to help me. I must keep the secret for him and protect him." I said.

"Hui Zhi, I can't give you the money." Teacher Lou began to shake his head. "I can't take in the risk of losing such a big sum. It's half of my whole life savings."

On the way back to his home, we started arguing. I stayed there for about an hour pleading with him to trust me, but my efforts failed. In the end, we reached the agreement that if I could give him material things of equivalent value as collateral, he would give me the cash. He would hold the items until I paid back the loan. After we agreed, I went home as quickly as I could pedal my old bicycle.

I went upstairs with such loud and hurried stomping, I must have sounded like a bull on the loose. My mother was in her room, she looked up with irritation.

"Mother! I have bad news! Someone had betrayed me

and the Canadian embassy wants to stop me from entering Canada!"

My mother frowned.

"But I have the passport anyway. If I don't leave tomorrow morning, I will likely never have the chance to go again. I booked the ticket, but I needed five thousand renminbi. Teacher Lou has already taken the cash from his bank but he needs insurance so that he will feel safe in lending it to me. Can you give me your bankbook with five thousand renminbi in it? I need to give it to him and let him hold it for a while."

My mother stared at me silently.

"Mother, if you want me to leave home, this is the only way. I have promised that I will pay back the money to Teacher Lou as soon as possible. I will also mail you some money. I will do my best."

My mother's face radiated reluctance. "By the way you ran upstairs, I already knew that there was some emergency," she said. Then she said, "Okay."

I took her bankbook, ran from home like the wind, and pedalled back over to Teacher Lou's house. When I arrived, I wrote a note acknowledging that I had borrowed the five thousand renminbi in cash and gave him my mother's bankbook as a guarantee that he would get the money back from me. If I didn't repay the money within six months, he could ask my mother for the money, since he held her bankbook. I had the five thousand in my hands but it was now seven thirty. I rushed to the international air ticket building, but of course it was closed.

I walked along the dark, quiet hallway hoping to find someone working late who could give me information on how to contact a ticket officer.

"Hey, what are you doing here?" A man's voice came from

behind me. I turned and saw an elderly security guard holding a flashlight in his left hand and a walkie-talkie in his right.

"I'm looking for a ticket salesman," I answered.

"Everyone is finished work." The guard gave me a suspicious look. His eyes searched me from head to toe. Then his voice softened a little. Perhaps I wasn't a thief. "Come back tomorrow morning at eight o'clock."

"But my ticket is already booked!" I wailed. "My flight leaves tomorrow morning at eight o'clock!"

"Well, little comrade, I can't help you. I'm just the security guy for the night. Go home to sleep and figure it out tomorrow." He walked away.

I didn't go home but continued to check each office to see if I could find someone who might have stayed late. There was absolutely no one in the building except the security guard and me. Finally I gave up the search and started to cry. I was at the end of my wits, and there was nothing else I could do. After an hour, the security guard completed his patrol circle and saw that I had still not left.

"Why are you still here?" he demanded. "I told you to go home."

"No, my ticket is in here. I need to leave tomorrow at eight A.M. Please help me! Please!" I continued to weep.

The guard shook his head. "This girl is stubborn, very stubborn," he mumbled. He walked away again.

About three hours passed, and the security guard saw me again and again. I remained in the same place, still crying hard, whenever he circled around the building. At about ten thirty, he finally stopped again and asked me for the details of my ticket. "Are you sure that you bought a ticket here and must leave tomorrow morning?"

"Yes! I'm not lying to you. I bought a first class ticket, but

I didn't have enough cash with me at the time. I went to the bank to get the money, but when I returned, the office was closed. I have to pick up my ticket tonight, because the plane leaves tomorrow morning."

The security guard used his wireless phone and made a call. "Hello, Manager Wong? There's a young woman here who says she has a ticket waiting for her in the office. She says that her flight will leave tomorrow morning. She's been here in tears for almost three hours. Can you come here to solve the problem?"

Half an hour later, a middle-aged woman arrived on a bicycle. She opened the office and turned on a computer to search. She soon found my name. The computer confirmed that I had booked the first class ticket from Shanghai to Toronto with stops in Tokyo and Vancouver. The flight would take off in the morning at eight o'clock. "Do you know which salesperson booked your flight? I don't have individual staff keys to open the drawers," the manager said. I tried my best to describe the young salesman. The manager thought it sounded like a man named Xiao Min.

"You'll come to his home with me to verify that he's the right person," Manager Wong said.

As we rode through the streets on our bikes, a sudden heavy rain fell, soaking us both to the skin. When we arrived at Xiao Min's home, he was asleep. Manager Wong roused him and I recognized him as my salesman. The three of us went back to the office on our bicycles. Xiao Min opened his drawer and handed my ticket to me.

I thanked everybody who'd helped me so much and hurried home. I still had to pack and get to the airport. I stopped at a twenty-four hour drug store and spent my last ten renminbi on some medicine for stomach pain and fever. I planned to take it with me to Canada, because I didn't have the money to buy medical insurance and see doctors if I fell ill.

When I arrived home, it was one o'clock in the morning, and my mother had gone to bed. I walked very quietly to my room on the third floor and started packing my two suitcases. I put all of my clothing in one suitcase and all the gifts in the other, then when I'd finished packing, I started writing letters. The first letter was to the agent, Lao Ho. I thanked him profusely for taking such a risk in giving me the passport. I told him that I would leave that morning, and as soon as I arrived in Canada, I would give him a call. The second letter was to the factory manager, in which I asked him to allow me a temporary absence for the next six months because I had to go overseas to visit a relative. The third letter was to my mother.

> Dear Mother,
>
> Thanks for lending me your bankbook to give to Teacher Lou. When I arrive in Toronto, I will let you know. If I can get into Canada, please help me by mailing this letter to the factory, but only when you have heard from me. Since I don't know how long I will be able to stay in Canada, I must keep my job open until I know whether I have the chance to stay there. Please take care of yourself and goodbye.
>
> P.S. I have left the front door key and the key to my room here for you.

When I'd finished all the things I could think of doing, it was four o'clock in the morning. It was time to go, since I had to take three different buses to get to the airport. I kissed my keys before placing them on the table. My tears dripped onto the keys and the letters. I had lived in this house for thirty-four years, three months and twenty-one days since the day

I was born. I had a deep affection for it. Finally, I took the two suitcases and one handbag and walked slowly and quietly down to the ground floor. I closed our front door. "Goodbye, my mother," I said. "Goodbye, my home."

I still loved them.

After a two hours journey, I arrived at the Shanghai airport just two hours before the plane was to depart. I had not eaten since a light breakfast the previous morning, and I hadn't slept at all. I looked for somewhere to buy some food, but it was too early for the stores to be open. When I boarded my flight, I was looking forward to a big meal but it was a short trip to Japan and we were served only small bag of peanuts with tea and juice. When the plane landed in Tokyo I went in search of food. I looked around the airport to find something reasonably priced, but the food was extremely expensive: even a little sandwich cost five hundred yen. I went to the washroom to drink water, which would temporarily make my stomach feel full. I held sixty U.S. dollars but knew nothing about the exchange rates and did not realize that I could afford something.

I went to the check-in desk to claim my seat on the flight to Vancouver. The woman at the counter said in English, "I can't find a seat for you. Your ticket is not valid." I didn't understand her, because my English was very limited. Luckily, two Chinese students who were going to study in Vancouver and who were on the same flight that I was supposed to take, volunteered to translate for me.

"How could this be?" I said in surprise. "Look! My ticket says from Tokyo to Vancouver, and from Vancouver to Toronto." I showed my ticket to the two students.

"When did you buy this ticket?" the check-in woman asked me through the students.

"Yesterday."

"Tickets for this flight were all booked at least two months in advance or even longer, so how can you have bought it yesterday? The computer doesn't show that you bought this ticket. No wonder it isn't working," she said. "Next, please!"

I held on to the two students, pleading with them to help me get more information. They found out that my luggage would go to Vancouver as scheduled, but I must stay in the Tokyo airport and put my name on a waiting list for the next available flight. There were already about ten people ahead of me who had been waiting for a last-minute check-in. I would need to wait at least a week to get onto a flight.

I didn't have enough money to stay in Tokyo or for food, and my luggage was going on to Vancouver without me with all of the things I had bought with my twelve years of savings. The Canadian embassy in Beijing would now have enough time to call the Vancouver immigration office and ask them to prevent me from entering Canada.

Desperate, I went to another check-in desk and showed them my ticket. "Look." I pointed at it. Then I pointed at myself and said, "No money, no English." The gentleman smiled and shook his head. I repeated the same thing at every check-in desk, and everyone refused.

I was hungry again and went back to the washroom to fill my stomach with water. I went back and repeated the same words and the same story over and over again, making a circle of all of the check-in desks, hoping that someone would change their mind.

I had arrived at the Tokyo airport at nine in the morning, and it was now three in the afternoon. The two Chinese students flying to Canada came to say goodbye to me, because it was close to the flight time, and they had to go. I stood beside the gate watching them board the plane that I should have been on. The public address system announced that the plane would close off boarding in ten minutes. I ran to a corner, where I started crying. I cried so hard, I began to vomit. Since there was no food inside my stomach, I was throwing up yellow liquid with an awful sour taste. I went down on my knees in the corner, calling to God to help me.

I heard an urgent voice. "Miss! Wake up, miss!" I felt someone pulling on my sleeve, but the voice seemed to come from far away. "Let's go, miss!"

I opened my eyes and saw a tall black man pulling on my left arm. He made me run with him. He held a walkie-talkie in his left hand and spoke to somebody. We ran and ran. Suddenly I found myself aboard a plane and a moment later I was sitting in a seat. Around me, people applauded to welcome me aboard. I was the last person on. They closed the door. My prayers had been answered and my trials seemed over.

I had never been on an airplane in my life but was exhausted and starved. I hardly noticed as the jet accelerated down the runway and lifted off. Around me in the first class section, the flight attendants were serving wonderful looking food, but since I only knew a few English words including "fish," "please" and "tea," I got only fish and tea. The person sitting next to me had wine, champagne, beef, chocolates, dessert and fruit. The sight of this feast made me still hungrier but I finally fell asleep. When I awoke, I had a chill and a stomach ache and started vomiting again. I put my mouth to the paper bag and a flight attendant brought me a glass of water and a wet hand towel. She touched my forehead "Oh miss," she said. "You have a fever!" I recognized the word "doctor" on the public address system and at some point a doctor came and checked me over, then gave me two pills. I slept a bit, drank lots of water and ate some more fish. After what seemed an eternity, the plane began to descend and I began vomiting again. The flight attendant brought me another wet towel and used sign language to ask me to stay in my seat. When all the other passengers had left the plane, she held my arm and helped me to walk slowly off to a wheelchair.

A woman was waiting at the exit ramp and she pushed me over to the immigration office, where they found an interpreter. I was appreciative but I had a new worry: Vancouver immigration might refuse me entry into Canada.

The immigration officer put a three-month visitor visa stamp on my passport and told me I could extend for another three months if I wanted. It was as simple as that. A Chinese woman pushed my wheelchair to the luggage area. She asked me to identify my two suitcases, and she pulled them off the conveyor. She told me that another person would help me board the plane to Toronto. She also asked for Aunty Lui's phone number so that she could call her and inform her of my arrival time. She hoped that Aunty Lui would pick me up when I arrived at Pearson Airport.

As I sat in the wheelchair watching all of these strangers helping me voluntarily, I imagined that I had entered the country Karl Marx describes in his book, Das Kapital: the highest level of Communist life, in which people love each other, help each other and share with each other. But I was experiencing this in Canada, which was not a Communist country. I pinched my leg hard to make sure this was all real.

On the night of August 24th, 1985, I landed in Toronto.

7 Obedience to Masters

Summer, 1985

Aunty Lui was nowhere to be seen. An airport staff member helped me hail a taxi and gave the driver my aunt's home address in a place called Don Mills. She told him I didn't speak English and had only American money and the driver agreed to charge me twenty U.S. dollars. Upon our arrival, he pushed the doorbell to make sure that he had taken me to the right place. I heard a dog barking loudly. A man opened the door.

"I am Song Hui Zhi from China," I said in Chinese. "I am looking for Aunty Lui."

"Mommy! Hui Zhi is here!" he called.

Aunty Lui, a slightly stooped woman of about sixty, came out to welcome me in Cantonese. She introduced her sister, her daughter, her son-in-law who had opened the door for me, and her grandchildren. After I had given them the gifts I had brought from China and taken a shower, I went to the basement to sleep.

The next day, Aunty Lui informed me that the immigration

office in Toronto had called her to ask if I had arrived and that she suspected I must have been a criminal in China. The only way to stay legally in Canada, she informed me, was to marry a Canadian citizen. She had already found a single man for me but, in the meantime, I was to work as a maid. For my own good, she would train me how to become a qualified maid. I must cook three meals a day for her family and learn to use her vacuum cleaner. In the afternoon, my job would be to iron the clothing she had already piled up like a small mountain in the basement. She forbade me ever to touch the TV or stereo, because they were expensive. She paused to let this all sink in. Then she pointed to the dog.

"This dog's life is more important than yours," she explained. "You come from mainland China and your value here is less than a Canadian dog."

My feelings of gratitude for her help evaporated with this wound to my dignity.

I called the immigration office. The man who answered said they just wanted to know where I was so they could relay the information to Beijing. I also needed to make calls to my mother and to agent Lao Ho to confirm I had arrived safely.

"That's too expensive," Aunty Lui said. "You can use the telegraph service to tell your mother of your arrival. You can change your U.S. money into Canadian quarters to make a long distance call to the agent from the payphone on the street."

I called Lao Ho in Shanghai from the payphone near Aunty Lui's house. I had difficulty understanding the operator's English, but I somehow managed it. I told Lao Ho how much I appreciated his help. Since I was now in Canada, I told him to blame me for the entire situation so as not to jeopardize his position.

Summer, 1985

I remained in Aunty Lui's house for two weeks, working as her maid. If she needed to go out, I had to leave the house too. Since she didn't trust me, I had to wait on the street for her return so I would not steal her things. The wonderful country in which I had been received on that first day in the airport had vanished as soon as I met Aunty Lui. I was hurt, sad and lonely.

A week after my arrival, Aunty Lui introduced me to a tall man who worked at the Sheraton hotel as a doorman. She wanted me to marry him, stay in Canada and help her in her old age. I met the doorman, whose name was John, in Chinatown at a restaurant, along with Aunty Lui and her friend, who was acquainted with John already. I then met him alone a second time at another Chinese restaurant. After lunch, he took me to a Chinese movie theatre. It was showing a pornographic movie made in Thailand I felt insulted and demeaned. I sat there for about half an hour, until I couldn't take it any more, then I walked out. He got up and ran after me.

"How dare you to take me to watch such a dirty movie?" I demanded. "I never, ever want to see you again!"

"I didn't know that it was a sex movie," he claimed weakly.

"Please don't call me again. We're finished!" I took the transit back to Aunty Lui's house.

Aunty Lui told me that she couldn't find me job as a maid, because though she'd showed my photo to several of her friends who needed a babysitter, they all thought that I was overqualified, and too attractive to be a babysitter and maid. I'd have to find a job myself and she warned me that I would have to lie about my visa limit and say that it was good for a year, not three months, or no one would want to hire me. I didn't want to lie, but I needed a job. After thinking it over, I decided that I wouldn't volunteer to tell the truth of the visa term, but if an employer asked for it, I would tell them.

I read the classified section in the Chinese newspaper and made many calls. At first no one wanted me, since I only had a three-month visa, and I had no children of my own. Eventually a lady named Mrs. Wong wanted to interview me. When I arrived in the lobby of her apartment building in downtown Toronto near the Eaton Centre, I saw a Filipina woman leaving. Mrs. Wong asked me a few questions then said that I could start work at her home the next day. She told me that she liked my honesty and she only needed a maid for a short time, because she was waiting for her chauffeur in Hong Kong to come to Canada. The immigration process would take three to five months. She was experienced enough to know that I could easily get an extension from the immigration office.

I started working for Mrs. Wong as a maid and babysitter after I had been in Canada for two weeks, and it quickly became clear that her family was rich. Her husband had businesses in Hong Kong and travelled a lot, and her son Phil was studying at a boarding school called Appleby in a nearby town called Oakville. Every day I started work at seven in the morning preparing breakfast for Kim, Mrs. Wong's nine-year-old, then took the child to school by taxi. I did all the housework, cleaned the apartment, did the laundry, shopped, and cooked. In the afternoon, I picked Kim up from school and made dinner, then washed dishes until seven P.M. Mrs. Wong paid me five hundred dollars cash per month for twelve hours a day of work, six days a week, and allowing me to eat and sleep in her home. I was delighted with the salary. In two months, I'd be able to pay back Teacher Lou, as I had promised.

The housework was not difficult and I even had some free time. After I took Kim to school by taxi, I walked back to the apartment and walked back again to pick her up in the afternoon, to save Mrs. Wong cab fare. I always held the child's hand, but she seemed uninterested in my good intentions. At such times, I thought of the close relationship I'd had with my own babysitter and how she'd held my hand on the way to school.

The most difficult part of being a maid was that I had to swallow my pride and obey my employer in everything. It reminded me of our maids and how they'd always responded to my mother's orders with "Yes, Madam," and a bow. Now that I had to do the exactly the same thing, it was hard to handle. Every evening after seven, as soon as I finished work, I disappeared into my own bedroom. After twelve hours of work, it was the only time that I could take off my mask and be myself. I wrote entries into my diary every night and told myself that one day I would shine like a diamond. I copied famous quotes and pinned them on the bedroom wall to encourage myself to never give up on my goals.

After I'd worked at Mrs. Wong's home for about five weeks, I received a letter from a friend named Pan Ping, whom I had met in Shanghai when we'd been interviewed by the Canadian embassy official on the same day. She was visiting family in Vancouver. She told me that she knew of a single man who was looking for a wife. He was a Chinese Canadian named Sam. She told me that he was a sea captain. Because his job had an irregular schedule, and he spent a lot of time on the ship, he'd had difficulty finding a wife. She asked me to come to Vancouver to meet him. It was a golden opportunity now that he had ten days shore leave.

I imagined what this captain, who Pan Ping described as having a lot of education and managing a huge ship, must be like. He would have a big heart and much self-confidence. I decided I couldn't miss this great chance, as my friend had said, so I told Mrs. Wong about it and asked if I could go to Vancouver for a week. She said that she would give me three days to meet the captain, and if we liked each other, he could come to visit me in Toronto later.

Mrs. Wong helped me buy a return ticket to Vancouver, since I didn't have five hundred dollars for airfare (my first month's salary having been mailed to Teacher Lou). She said she didn't mind paying me in advance for the next month.

When I arrived at Vancouver Airport, Pan Ping and her brother were there to pick me up. I was so happy to see her; it was the first time I had laughed since I had arrived in Canada. On the way to her brother's home, Pan Ping told me that Sam was excited to meet me, and I would be staying at his home. "What? I will sleep at a single man's home? No, my friend, I don't think that's a good idea," I said.

"Sam is a gentleman," Pan Ping replied. "He will not touch you or take advantage of you at all. He promised this already. He owns a two-bedroom condo and has never had anyone in his guest room. He bought new bedding and new pyjamas for you. Oh, Hui Zhi, I'm so excited for you. I hope you and Sam like each other. I would love having you in Vancouver with me."

I met Sam at a restaurant that same day. He was of medium height and build. His demeanour was serious, but he seemed nervous. After dinner, I went to his home with him. He showed me my bedroom and washroom then said goodnight. The next morning, I got up very early, brushed my teeth, and made my bed then just sat there waiting for him to get up. When he did, and we had breakfast together, we started to talk. We chatted about of our families, our education and our personal interests. I learned that he was a coxswain, whose job it was to steer a ship, but he was not a captain. The ship took merchandise between Vancouver and Mexico.

Everything was friendly until I mentioned that I be leaving on Sunday, because my employer had only agreed that I could have three days off. Sam was upset at this news. "Only three days?" he said. "How can you expect me to make a big decision in such a short time?"

"Please calm down," I said. "I didn't expect you to make any decision at all. We both live in Canada and we still can visit each other as friends." But Sam just kept repeating the same words over and over. There was no room for further discussion. I didn't know what to do and sat in silence for hours. Finally I decided to call Pan Ping for help.

After she arrived, I told her what had happened, and she advised me to stay longer in Vancouver. "Hui Zhi, don't you see that staying here and making Sam happy is your most important priority? If you married him, you could stay in Canada legally and have a husband with a stable salary. Why do you worry about this responsibility to your employer? Why should you care about her? Does she care about you? If she does, then why did she give you only three days off?"

I didn't totally agree with her, but I agreed to call a woman named Jean Chan whom I'd met at a library in Toronto. Jean worked in a clothing factory. I asked if she could take a week off and take my place at Mrs. Wong's home. I told her that I'd happily pay the week's salary that she would lose from the factory. But Jean had already used her week of vacation.

I told Pan Ping that I had no other option and I that had to go back to Toronto the next day as promised. I hoped that Sam would see me as a responsible person, and I hoped that he would realize that I hadn't intended to force him to make such an important decision in such a short time. In fact, I was in no hurry to make a big decision myself. I could visit him again, and I welcomed him to visit me. Pan Ping tried to help convey this message to him, but no matter what she said, Sam just repeated, "How can I make a decision in three days? No, I can't. I just can't marry her in three days." again and again. He seemed a narrow-minded person and I wondered how I could marry him and share my life with him. Marriage requires love, respect, understanding, care, and sharing. Pan Ping, meanwhile, a disappointed matchmaker, implied that I should lower my standards because I needed to immigrate legally to Canada. I grew increasingly uncomfortable and depressed.

I had been treated unfairly in China, and I told myself that I shouldn't bend to anyone or allow them to offend my dignity in this, my second life. Therefore, I told her that although Sam might be a good man, I wasn't interested in dating him. In the meantime, I hoped she would allow me to stay at her home on Saturday night, and I would leave on Sunday. She said that her brother didn't have a spare bedroom, but I could sleep in hers, if I didn't mind sleeping on the floor.

On Sunday, I flew back to Toronto. As I sat on the plane, I wept again. This trip had cost me so much money, time, and emotional energy.

Life went on in Mrs. Wong's home much as before until one day I heard her crying while talking with her husband on the phone. I didn't know the cause but I felt sorry for her. I'd had enough sorrowful experiences myself. I gently handed her a few tissues.

After she hung up, I spoke a few words to her and she told me that she found it difficult looking after two children without her husband, and living in this new country with its totally different culture, language, customs, and its cold winters. She told me that sometimes she felt like jumping onto the subway tracks. I was shocked to hear that she'd had such suicidal inclinations.

To try to help her, I told her about some of my own dark periods, and how I'd come to Canada looking for a better future. I shared the story of Abraham Lincoln's difficult life with her and told her that whenever I felt down, it was his story that inspired me. Lincoln had failed at almost everything he'd tried, from business to political life. I believed that the pain had made him a better person, in that he had more ability to empathize and to be compassionate. His failures had made him stronger and more persistent.

After that, Mrs. Wong and I became friends. She told me to call her by her first name, Rose, and took me to see a man named Mr. Green, who was reputed to be the most successful immigration lawyer in Canada. She hoped that he could find a legal way for me to stay in Canada. Because of my background, Mr. Green suggested that I try to find a doctor of alternative medicine who would hire me through the government manpower department. He felt that since I had studied Chinese medicine and acupuncture, I would have a good chance of getting a work permit from the immigration office. It brought me new hope, so Rose and I started to search for a suitable doctor.

Through a mutual friend of Rose's, Mr. Yi, a chiropractor, expressed interest in hiring me. He was a medical doctor from Singapore who had studied in Toronto for four more years to become a chiropractor. He had two clinics in the city, one in North York near his home and the other in the Eaton Centre. Doctor Yi wanted me to provide my educational documents and to meet me personally before making a decision.

The next Wednesday evening at six o'clock, Doctor Yi

finished his work and walked across the street to Rose's apartment. I met him in the lobby. Rose was out for dinner with some friends, and I'd brought Kim into the lobby with me. The interview took about an hour, and Doctor Yi said he'd be happy to hire me if I could get a work permit. Hiring me would allow him to offer his patients more services. Rose loaned me a thousand dollars to pay Mr. Green a deposit for getting me a work permit. With his help, my future seemed bright.

I was grateful to Rose and didn't feel so bad about being her maid any more. We had a lot in common. We shared a love of art, music, classic novels and opinions about Chinese politics. She told me that her father-in-law had been a successful businessman in Hong Kong, a major shareholder in a bank and a railway and that he had donated a lot of money to China for the building of new hospitals and schools. Because of his influence, she'd had many chances to visit China, and she had developed a keen understanding of the mainland. "I hired you because you are an honest Chinese," she said. "Even though I lived in Hong Kong, and it's under British rule, I'm still Chinese, and my heart leans toward China." I was touched by her patriotism.

We lived happily together after that. Sometimes she taught me English, and sometimes we sang together. One afternoon, when I returned from grocery shopping, I heard the sounds of clacking pottery coming the dining room. I found Rose and Kim with their heads on the dining room table, pretending to sleep. On the table were three bowls of Chinese dessert. I decided to ignore their fake sleeping and pretended to eat the dessert. I deliberately scratched the bowl loudly with the spoon and said, "Well, what a delicious dessert. Since everybody is sleeping, I've had the chance to eat it all. Yum and yum." Rose and Kim couldn't keep silent any longer; they started to laugh, then all three of us laughed heartily together. The little apartment was filled with joy.

Shortly after, Rose told me that her husband was coming to Toronto. The day Mr. Wong arrived, she went to the airport to pick him up while I stayed at home to cook dinner. Rose told me that her husband enjoyed food made of soybeans cut very fine, and I was happy to spend extra time to please him. During the dinner, the four of us sat at the dining table together, and we even drank some good wine. Unfortunately, Mr. Wong was very surprised and unhappy to see that his wife was treating her maid like a friend. That night, I heard them arguing about it. In the end, Mr. Wong convinced Rose to fire me because I'd left Kim in the lobby for an hour during my meeting with Doctor Yi. Even though I'd kept an eye on her the whole time, from Mr. Wong's point of view, this "neglect" showed that I wasn't responsible enough to care for his daughter.

They arranged for Rose's mother to come to Toronto and replace me until their chauffeur could come. The day I left, Rose was cold to me. She told me that she didn't want me as a friend any more and that she didn't want me to contact her in the future. As I left, I moved a foot towards her and thought of giving her a hug, but she dropped her eyes to the floor to avoid meeting mine. I turned back to the door and ran to the elevator. As soon as the elevator's door closed, I cried again.

With my two suitcases in hand, I took a taxi to the house of another family. I'd found them in the Chinese newspaper's classified section. I started working as a maid and babysitting for them on the very same day that I left Rose's place. Meanwhile, I waited for my work permit so I could work for Dr. Yi.

Chapter Seven

My new job was in the home of a working class Mandarin-speaking Chinese family. The husband, David, had come from Guangzhou and worked in a factory in a suburb of Toronto. After a few years, he had returned to China to marry his girlfriend Amy and sponsor her to come to Canada. They'd had two girls after the marriage. One, named Jean, was six years old and in Grade One, and the other child, Ann, was four and attended half-days in the local kindergarten. When Ann was a year old, Amy had started work as a waitress in a Chinese restaurant. They both worked extremely hard. David worked from eight A.M. to eight P.M. with additional commuting time, and Amy worked from ten A.M. to eleven P.M. at the restaurant. I rarely saw them at home from the time I got up at seven A.M. until nine P.M., after I put the two girls to sleep and went to my own room on the third floor.

The long working hours was the reason they had problems finding people to work for them at low pay and long hours. They accepted my temporary offer to work until I received my work permit. Since the parents were not available for their children, I felt I had a responsibility to look after those girls as though I were their own mother.

Every morning, I got the children up early, as Ann needed me to dress her. Then the three of us had breakfast together. After that, I held their hands as I walked them to their schools. It only took me a couple of days to realize that those girls hadn't received any early childhood education from their parents. I decided to teach them a bit at home in addition to just being a maid and babysitter. I taught them to wash their little hands before meals or after using the toilet, I taught them to never lie if they made a mistake, I taught them singing and dancing in the evening. After dinner, I checked Jean's homework and read a children's book to them. Jean and Ann got used to having a shower before bed. Jean could manage independently most of the time, but I had to bathe Ann every night, and sometimes I sang her a lullaby before she fell asleep in my arms.

About two-thirty in the morning, after I'd been with this family for ten days, I was awakened by the loud sound of arguing coming from the master bedroom. I put my clothes on and ran to the room. When I arrived, I saw David holding scissors, cutting hair from the front of Amy's head, while screaming at her, "I'm making you look ugly! So you can't go out fooling around with those rich men any more!" I grabbed the scissors from his hand, and I saw that Amy had picked up the phone.

"Who are you calling at two-thirty in the morning?" I asked.

"The police," Amy answered.

"Why?"

"It will help me divorce him faster if he's holding a pair of scissors," she said.

"The scissors are in my hand now," I pointed out to her. "You aren't in danger. I suggest that you two calm down first, then figure the divorce situation out later."

Amy put the phone back down. I tried my best to calm them both and convinced Amy to sleep in my bedroom. I moved to the living room and slept on the sofa.

I didn't sleep well after that. Although I liked looking after their two cute girls, the situation was too risky for me with this family. Their relationship was too unstable, and if I stayed with them, I risked having my illegal working situation discovered. I decided to tell them my concerns and asked for their permission to leave. They agreed that I could leave in two weeks. Before I left, I had a long talk with David to try to make him understand that violence was no good for anyone, especially since the conflict would hurt the children. I asked him to promise that he wouldn't use violence any more, and suggested that they get professional help. I hoped that the next babysitter would care for their two innocent girls as much as I had.

My original plan was to keep looking for short-term work with a suitable family, but Doctor Yi had convinced me to work for him, even though I still did not have a work permit. He said, "Why are you wasting your talents working as a maid and babysitter?"

"I have no choice, Dr. Yi," I said. "As long as I haven't received a work permit, I must hide myself by working in a private home."

"How much do they pay you?" he asked.

"Five hundred dollars a month plus free meals and shelter," I replied.

"OK, you can work in my clinic, and I'll pay you the same amount in cash. Of course, you can eat and sleep at my house," he added.

And so I moved into Dr. Yi's house. This would be a good opportunity for me. I had now been in Canada about four months.

8 A Gypsy Winter

1986

Doctor Yi owned a spacious four-bedroom house on Finch Avenue in a respectable area of the city. After I moved into the house, I found out that he was divorced, with a daughter in her early twenties. There was a bedroom reserved for the daughter, though she never seemed to stay there.

As soon as I moved in, he told me that he'd changed his mind and wanted me to do domestic work for half the day and work at the clinic for the other half. I prepared breakfast for him every morning. After breakfast, he went to work at one of his clinics near his home. He would return home to eat shortly after noon, then after lunch he drove me to the Eaton Centre to work at the clinic there. All afternoon I did acupuncture and shiatsu massage until six, then I took the subway and bus back to his home by myself.

One day Dr. Yi asked for my opinion on how he could become well known in his profession. I suggested that he write a book. He thought this a great idea but soon turned things around and ordered me to write it for him. This I stumbled into the new and unwanted job of working on his book every evening. It was based on previous audio recordings that he had made, together with some old notes.

Usually I went to sleep around eleven P.M., before Doctor Yi arrived home. When he got home, he would often come into my bedroom without asking and tell me to report on my writing progress. Sometimes he would blather on about his opinions on medical cases and practice until two P.M. He criticized Western medicine for "poisoning" people and ranted that surgeons were murderers. He told me to put those criticisms into the book.

I felt unsafe to sleep in a room without a door lock, while living with a single man who controlled my life and on whom I depended for help getting a work permit to stay in Canada. I asked myself: "What should I do if he came to my bedroom to molest me? Should I fight? If I resist, would I lose the chance to stay in Canada?" I asked myself the same question over and over but couldn't find a good answer. My vulnerable situation made me fearful. Every night I slept in my clothes so that I would be prepared to get up whenever I heard a suspicious noise. Often I would jump up out of bed when I heard Dr. Yi open my bedroom door. Eventually I could no longer allow myself to sleep. After two weeks of working more than twelve hours a day and refusing to sleep at night, I nearly had a nervous breakdown. I desperately needed help.

I had been introduced to a Chinese student named Michael Zhou. Michael was looking for a girlfriend and hoped to immigrate to Canada through marriage. Michael had a one-year student visa with his sister and brother in-law as his sponsors. After we met, I confided in him that I was older than he was and only had a visitor's visa myself. Michael and I had come from the same country and the same city in similar circumstances. We understood each other and have kept up our friendship ever since. One day I called him and told him about my vulnerable situation and concerns about living alone in Doctor Yi's house. He asked his sister Janice if I could sleep temporarily in her apartment to get me out of my plight. She agreed.

I told Doctor Yi that a friend's family had invited me to live with them, and that I wanted to move out of his home but keep working in his clinic. I was tremendously relieved when he agreed.

Janice lived in a two-bedroom apartment in Scarborough, the most easterly of the communities of metro Toronto. I moved there in the middle of December, 1985, less than two months before the Chinese New Year. Janice and her husband got up at seven-thirty every morning and went to sleep at eleven. Since she'd been kind enough to allow me to sleep on the couch at her living room, I tried to disturb their life as little as possible. I always waited until 10:55 P.M. to press the button asking her to let me into the building and quietly left her home five minutes before they got up.

On the Chinese New Year eve, I arrived at her building at the usual time, but no one answered my ring, and I didn't have a key. I waited outside in the cold for three hours. I was chilled through, so I paced back and forth in a circle and jumped up and down to keep myself warm. At last, at about two o'clock in the morning, I saw Michael and Janice and her husband returning home.

"Oh, Hui Zhi!" Janice exclaimed. "I'm so sorry that I forgot to tell you we were going to a New Year party. We just kept dancing!"

The next morning, I was sick with a fever, sore throat, and

a cough. Michael helped me move into his bedroom to rest and recover. Since I didn't have medical insurance, I couldn't see a doctor. I had some medicine for fever that I had brought from China, but I didn't have cough medicine. I wrote down the name of the Chinese medicine I needed for my cough and asked Michael to buy it for me in Chinatown. When he returned and handed me a glass of water and the medicine, I started to weep. I was touched by his caring and was feeling sorry for myself. I heard his sister calling.

"Michael, come out. I want to talk to you!"

When he went to her, I could hear her upset tone coming from the living room.

"Why is she crying? Is she complaining that I wasn't nice to her? Tell her to move back to Doctor Yi's home. He's rich and owns such a big house. She doesn't have to live in my apartment! I'm a poor woman."

I left her apartment the next morning and never bothered Janice after that. I called Aunty Lui to ask if she would let me sleep in their basement again. I explained that although I was working for Doctor Yi at his clinic with five hundred dollars per month payment agreement, but I hadn't yet received any money from him. I was facing homelessness.

Aunty Lui refused. "This house belongs to my daughter. I can't let you sleep in her basement. If you become a refugee, Hui Zhi, I will find you and ask Canadian immigration to deport you back to China."

It was the middle of January, 1986. I was homeless and started living a gypsy lifestyle, moving from place to place, trying to make do day by day. I called a list of people to offer my acupuncture and shiatsu service in exchange for leftover food and for allowing me to sleep on their sofa for the night. Sometimes I only had to make a couple of calls before I found a place to stay, but sometimes it took much longer. Every day, the uncertainty of finding a place to sleep in the cold Canadian winter left me frightened and exhausted.

When I walked through the Eaton Centre to Doctor Yi's clinic, I passed many stores. A bakery caught my eye—the beautiful cakes and delicious chocolates were so tempting. When I stopped to look at them, it stimulated my appetite so much I had to swallow my saliva. Then I recalled that after my father had passed away, my mother had shown no interest in celebrating my birthday. I remembered buying a cake and a half pound of dark chocolate for my thirtieth birthday. That night, I'd stayed up until morning to read *The Fallen Woman* and ate the whole cake and all of the chocolate. Now I vowed that one day, when I had money, I would do this for myself once again.

I kept walking and stopped to peer into an electronics store. A colour TV caught my attention when I saw the image of a criminal in a Canadian jail. He had a small room with a single bed, toilet and sink. It looked much better living in that jail than in my own world of freedom. I wondered I should somehow break the law and live in jail and not worry about where to sleep every night. I went to the police station at Dundas and University Avenue and tried to explain but nobody there could understand me.

On February 25th, 1986, I only had seventy-five cents and my Metro pass left. The first three months of pay from Rose Wong was all gone. The first two month's wages I'd paid back to Teacher Lou, and I'd used a month's salary for the Vancouver trip. The last four hundred dollars that I'd made at the second family's place had been spent during the last two months to feed myself. The seventy-five cents in my pocket was only enough for three phone calls to find a person who would exchange my medical services for dinner and a place for me to sleep. Two of the three prospects didn't want my services and nobody answered the phone at the last place. I didn't know what to do. My last hope was that the family that hadn't answered my call would come home late and agree to barter with me. I had no quarters left to make another phone call, so I decided to go there, though Scarborough was far away.

When I arrived at their home, I pushed the doorbell, but no one answered. I waited and waited, but no one came home. It was about ten P.M., and I was famished, weary and disappointed. I wept for about half an hour, then decided to go back to the downtown police station and ask for help. On the way back, I got lost. I turned from one small street to another and couldn't figure out how to get back to the main street to catch the bus. Everyone said it was exceptionally cold that February—minus 20 C and with the wind-chill it felt like minus 40 C. I walked on and on in the dark and cold with an empty stomach. I felt the cold from my feet and hands move up my legs and arms. Gradually it spread to my chest towards my heart. My entire body was nearly frozen, and only my brain still functioned well. I felt death creeping up on me. I knew that I was dying. I didn't cry at that moment. I thought, "Hui Zhi, yes, your life will end tonight. But you did your best. You tried and tried very hard."

At a corner, I noticed that a car had stopped at a stop sign. I'd never hitched a ride in my life, but at that moment I felt myself to be at the crossroads of life and death. I knocked on the window. It was an older Canadian couple. The wife opened the door and let me in. After I got into the car and sat down on the back seat, the husband, who was driving, asked me where I was going. I started to cry again and couldn't talk. After ten minutes I felt my body start to tingle as the warmth of the car gradually replaced the cold.

"I don't know," I said through my tears. "I'm a homeless. I'm so cold and hungry. I thought I would die tonight."

I heard them talking quietly. They took me to their house and gave me a glass of milk and a few pieces of bread. They tried to talk to me but realized I didn't speak much English and simply pointed me towards the washroom and told me I could take a shower. As the warm water rinsed my body, I felt so good, I started crying again. This kind and generous couple let me sleep in their guestroom. It was the first time I had slept in a real bed for several months.

The next morning, after I had breakfast there, I gave them Dr. Yi's business card and tried to tell them that I worked at the clinic in the afternoon. If they needed any help, I would be happy to help them just as they had helped me. I tried to tell them how thankful I was, but I don't know how much they understood. One thing I am sure of: looking into my eyes, the wife understood the deep appreciation coming from the bottom of my heart.

After nearly freezing to death, I was extremely frightened. I realized that if I wanted to survive, I had to reach out for help, not just from within the Chinese community. I needed to involve myself in the Canadian community as well. After meeting those kind Canadians that night, I felt encouraged to contact more Canadian people, even though my English was so rudimentary.

I had a Canadian patient named Mary who was in her twenties and worked for a TV station. Her office was just two doors down from Dr. Yi's clinic. Mary had received several treatments from me, and every time she tried to pay me directly, until Dr. Yi stopped her and said she should pay him. Since Mary knew I didn't speak English well, she tried to teach me some words and make conversation with me during the treatments. I sensed that she was a kind and warmhearted person, and I decided to pay her a visit. I used my poor English and a lot of body language to explain my situation. As soon as Mary understood what was going on in my life, she gave me a tight hug. She told me to meet her at six in her office.

When I arrived at her office shortly after six, she was still busy talking to people. At six thirty, she closed the office and walked with me to the key duplication service in the mall. After she'd made a key, she took me to the food court for dinner. She gave me the key and told me that in the future, if I didn't have a place for the night, I could use this key and sleep on the sofa in her living room. She rented a two-bedroom apartment, which she shared with a roommate named Sherry. After dinner, Mary took me to the apartment in a part of Toronto called Cabbagetown to meet her roommate. I slept there that night.

That weekend, Mary introduced me to her boyfriend Robert, who worked for a yacht company as a salesman and manager. Robert shared a two-bedroom apartment with a roommate at Bathurst and St. Clair. He was a strong, well-built man with a big heart. He and Mary invited me to eat dinner with them and tried to ascertain which aspect of my life I needed the most help with. Robert showed me a secret key hidden under a rock outside his front door and told me that I was welcome to sleep in his apartment any time. Most weekends Mary spent time with Robert and slept at his apartment. Robert's apartment had a den with a sofa bed. He let me sleep in the den, which had a sliding door for privacy. I felt so fortunate at having met such kind and generous people.

After solving my shelter problem, I had to make some

money. Since I had left the babysitting work in December, I had not received a penny from Dr. Yi for all of the work I had done for him. I asked a few people if anyone wanted acupuncture or shiatsu that I could do by making house calls. My fee was only ten dollars for acupuncture and twenty dollars for an hour of shiatsu.

I got some private patients and customers outside Dr. Yi's clinic from time to time, which helped me survive. One evening I went to a Mr. Chang's home to do a house call. He owned a small home renovation business and wanted a one-hour shiatsu massage. It was my second visit. The first house call had taken place in the guest room, but this time he led me into his master bedroom. I noticed that there was no one else around that evening, and a TV and VCR sat atop a small table beside the bed.

Mr. Chang took his clothes off, leaving just his underwear and lay face down while I gave him the massage. After a half hour, he started to touch me. It made me nervous and I tried to move away. He turned over and asked me to watch the TV. He was playing a pornographic tape. It took me a few minutes to recognize it for what it was. I felt deeply embarrassed and turned my face away. Mr. Chang lunged at me, pushed me down onto the bed and tried to pull my clothes off. I started screaming and kicking. We were rolling and fighting on the bed, but somehow I found a chance to get up but he chased me and caught me near the sofa and forced me down onto it. We struggled again and again he tried to pull off my sweater and pants and lie on top of me. I fought back. I was filled with rage and that rage gave me tremendous energy. I screamed and kicked that devil, who had not provided himself with a weapon. At one point, I found my self on my feet and he was slow to rise. I ran away.

Chapter Eight

My arms and legs had been badly bruised but it never occurred to me to report the attack to the police. I was working illegally and knew now how vulnerable I was.

9 First Signs of Green

May, 1986

On the first of May, 1986, as I walked into the clinic, I was surprised to notice a new woman working there.

"Who is she?" I asked.

"She's a registered masseuse," Dr. Yi replied. "I hired her recently. I've waited for more than six months, and your lawyer still hasn't got you a work permit. I can't wait for you any longer. Why don't you marry somebody so you can stay in Canada legally?" He laughed. "I think marriage would be good for you. You can have some sex."

Dr. Yi hadn't fulfilled his agreement to help me get a work permit and hadn't paid me what he owed me, but I knew that I was powerless to argue with him, since my work permit application relied on his cooperation. I suspected he was upset at me because I wouldn't live at his house and only provided half days of free labour to him. Although I had worked for almost five months in his clinic and never received any money, it still was not enough for him. Now he showed his power over me:

He could threaten me any time he wanted.

The only recourse for me to stay permanently was through a marriage of convenience to a Canadian, just as Dr. Yi had said. But whom could I marry? I had lived in Canada for only a little more than eight months, and I didn't know many people. How could I find a suitable man? I thought of a few men I had socialized with. I knew that I would need a trustworthy and willing partner and that I would have to pay them a lot of money for their trouble.

In February, I had met Patrick, a sixty-three-year-old Irishman who worked on the railway. That day I'd been feeling hungry and drained of energy, because I hadn't eaten a proper meal for several days. As I walked through the Eaton Centre on the way to the clinic, I'd fainted in the middle of an escalator and fallen to the bottom. A few people surrounded me and tried to help me and Patrick was one of them. Later, after he'd put a bandage on my bleeding left leg, he took me to a restaurant for a proper lunch. Since that incident, we'd become friends. Patrick had a great passion for ballroom dancing. He'd hired me as his therapist when he was involved in a ballroom dance competition in Montreal. I shared a hotel room with his dance partner and dance teacher, Marisa.

Two and half months is only a short time, but I already knew that Patrick had a good heart. On the second of May I asked him if he would marry me on paper to help me to stay in Canada. His answer was, "Oh yes, Song, I'd be happy to take you for real as my darling wife."

I knew he liked me very much. Every time he met me in the shopping mall, he always called out, "Hi, sexy! Hi, smashing!" and would take an improvised dance step towards me. Although I knew that he was a kind man, I was embarrassed. I didn't want to be his real wife, and I didn't want to use him and hurt him. I remembered a few years before, when I'd advised my ex-husband to not use marriage to get immigration and so hurt your spouse. With regret, I took Patrick's name off my list.

Tom, a middle-aged divorced man, was my friend Robert's boss. Tom agreed to marry me on paper to help me to stay in Canada and wasn't even concerned about charging me a fee. I was so happy to have found him, but Robert warned me that I shouldn't trust him completely. He advised me to test Tom first by staying a night in his house to see if he would behave like a gentleman. I went to Tom's big house and sure enough, he insisted on sleeping with me I had to call Robert to pick me up. Through his ungentlemanly insistence on sleeping together, Tom had demonstrated that he couldn't be trusted to be a mere surrogate husband.

Christopher, a twenty-five year old Canadian man with a skin disease, had come to Dr. Yi's clinic a few months before for help. He didn't have a job or much education. Like me, he was a homeless person temporarily staying at a friend's apartment. He seemed to need money badly, so I offered him ten thousand dollars to marry me on paper and promised that I would pay the sum later. He accepted my offer.

On the sixth of May, Christopher and I went to the offices of the law firm Green and Spiegel. I wanted Mr. Green to know that Dr. Yi wouldn't let me work for him any more, and with no sponsor, this meant that I would have no a chance for a work permit. The only way for me to stay in Canada was to arrange to be married. When I went to the reception desk and asked to see Mr. Green, the receptionist, Rochelle, after looking at me curiously for a few moments, left her desk and went into the lawyer's office. After about ten minutes, she came back out with Linda, a Chinese secretary, Mrs. Wang.

"Mr. Green is not here," Linda told me in Chinese. "He's in Hong Kong on a business trip."

"Can I see another lawyer who can provide the document I need for a marriage?" I asked.

"No." Linda shook her head. "You can't get married now. You'll have to wait until Mr. Green comes back. He'll be back in Toronto in two days. You should come to see him alone."

I left, filled with disappointment.

Unknown to me, this Rochelle was an astute observer. As soon as I had walked in with Christopher, she'd figured out what I wanted. Normally it was not her business to get involved in any client's business, but it seems she felt sorry for me. She'd had Linda tell me in Chinese that I should delay my plan.

I returned to Mr. Green's office alone, as the secretary had instructed and Mr. Green greeted me warmly.

"Hi, Miss Song. Who's the lucky man who is going to marry you?" His voice was cheerful and his smile friendly.

"I don't have any choice, Mr. Green. Dr. Yi won't employ me any more."

"Don't worry about that Miss Song. I'll fix it for you. Do you have Dr. Yi's telephone number with you?"

He called the clinic. I didn't understand what he said on the call but when he hung up he said, "Mai wun-ti"—Chinese for "no problem." I learned later that he'd convinced Dr. Yi to reconsider his decision and to continue to sponsor me for a work permit.

A week later, I got a call to return to Mr. Green's office. When I arrived, I was told that he had arranged a work permit interview appointment for me in Los Angeles. I would have to leave Canada to apply for a work permit in Canada according to the country's immigration laws, but apparently Mr. Green had convinced Dr. Yi to reconsider his decision and sponsor me for a work permit.

"Where's Los Angeles?" I felt tears coming on. "How can I get there? How much will it cost?"

Mrs. Wang explained the details but I only had a hundred dollars in my wallet, I didn't speak English, and I didn't know how I could get to Los Angeles. It would be too difficult for me. I kept silent.

Mr. Green stepped into his secretary's office. "Are you happy to go to Los Angeles for a work permit interview?" he asked. He came closer and saw I was crying.

"Don't cry," he said. "I'll help you if you stop crying."

All of a sudden, I heard my dear father's voice in Mr. Green's words. I melted and cried even harder. What I did not know at this time was that Mr. Green had already booked a trip to Los Angeles to meet another client. He told his secretary to book me on the same flight and a hotel to match his Los Angeles schedule. On his advice, I called Christopher and explained that good fortune had come my way and we no longer needed to get married.

On Wednesday, May 28th, 1986, I arrived at the law office at one in the afternoon. After about ten minutes, Mr. Green came out and to my surprise drove me straight to Pearson Airport. It was only at this point that I learned that he would be accompanying me to Los Angeles. On one hand, I felt grateful and safe, but on the other I worried that I would owe him money that I wouldn't be able to repay.

Before boarding the flight, Mr. Green bought a few things in the duty-free store and asked me to choose a bottle of perfume. I felt shy and excited, because I'd never had perfume in my whole life. I looked around then picked the cheapest one.

During the five-hour flight, we chatted and got to know

each other better. It was difficult for both of us, because we didn't understand each other's language. But at least I understood that he was going to Los Angeles for a Hong Kong-based female client's interview. She'd paid Mr. Green's fare to Los Angeles, and I was getting mine from him for free. After we arrived in Los Angeles, he picked up a rental car and drove me to my downtown hotel.

It was a small three-star hotel that only charged forty dollars a night and had been reserved for me by Mr. Green's office. Mr. Green went to the reception desk and checked me in using his credit card then he handed me a room key.

"Your room is 402. Do you want me to go with you?"

"No, I can go by myself," I said. I blushed. I was acting like a five-year-old child, lost in the jungle, needing a babysitter at every step, rather than a thirty-five-year-old woman lost in the modern life of North America.

I found my room, put my stuff inside and went out into the street. I didn't venture too far, just far enough to find a store. I bought a green tie and a green handkerchief, then I went to a convenience store to buy a loaf of bread and a bunch of bananas for my meals. At the end of May, it was already hot in Los Angeles. I had seen an ice-making machine in the hotel, but I didn't know that ice was free. I drank the water from the washroom tap.

My interview was on Thursday afternoon at two P.M. and Mr. Green met me in the hotel lobby at noon to take me for lunch. In a fancy restaurant, I met the rich lady, Mrs. Ho, who had hired Mr. Green to obtain an interview for her with Canadian officials.

After we finished our delicious lunch, I gave him my little present. When he opened it, he just shook his head and said, "Silly girl...silly girl."

We walked a few blocks to the office where the interview was to take place. I was told to sit and wait patiently. After about an hour, Mr. Green came out and told me that everything was done and my work permit application was successful. I wouldn't have to marry anyone. The immigration officer handed me an application. When she found out that I didn't know much English, she filled the form out for me, told me to sign my name and pay eighty dollars. I did as she said and as I did I wondered why so many Canadians were being kind to me.

Before Mr. Green went back to his own hotel, he handed me a brochure for a tour of Disneyland and told me have some fun before returning home. "I don't think so," I said.

He took some bills from his pocket. "Here's a hundred dollars, Ms Song. Go have fun tomorrow."

"No!" I protested, "I don't want to spend your money."

"Please go, and pay me back later when you have money."

I did take the money, but I never went to Disneyland. I could not borrow money just to have fun. I didn't go to a restaurant to have a proper meal either. For those three days in Los Angeles, I hid in my hotel room with only some bread and bananas to eat. On Friday night, Mr. Green called to ask if I was okay. He told me that he would be leaving for Toronto the next morning. My own discount ticket required me to stay in Los Angeles for the weekend. Mr. Green said if I wanted, he would try to get me booked on his flight to leave with him on Saturday. And as usual, with his help, everything worked out.

When we arrived back in Toronto, we returned to his office, where I gave back his hundred dollars. He looked at me just as he had before and shook his head. "Silly girl," he said. "Silly girl."

10 Of Grandma

June 1986

After receiving my work permit, I thought I would be able to practice my profession at Dr. Yi's clinics, but it didn't work out. Monday afternoon I went downtown to Dr. Yi's clinic where the doctor and I were to discuss further arrangements now that I had my work permit. When I arrived, I was surprised to find a bouquet of flowers waiting for me. Attached was a letter from Christopher, which he'd delivered to the clinic personally while I was away. I opened the letter with mild trepidation.

> Dear Hui Zhi
> I love you very much but you've hurt me by not agreeing to marry me. You've broken your promise. I'm afraid, if you don't keep your promise, I'll have to kill you.
> Yours forever
> Christopher

I thought he'd understood. Perhaps the problem was my

poor English. Perhaps he wanted the money I had said I would pay for the marriage. No, no, I didn't want to believe he was actually a bad person.

In the end, I decided to give up working at Dr. Yi's clinic. It was the only place where Christopher could find me. I explained this to Dr. Yi, who seemed to understand, but I was sad anyway. I'd thought that now I'd be able to work at my profession legally and make good money. One day, I'd have my own apartment and three meals a day. Now I faced the prospect of returning to my gypsy life. As I was gathering my things, Mrs. Wang from Mr. Green's office called and asked me if I would go to the office the next morning.

When I arrived at Mr. Green's office the next morning, Mrs. Wang was waiting for me. She explained that Mr. Green's mother had undergone heart bypass surgery, been hospitalized for quite some time, and had just been released that weekend. She needed someone to look after her. Mr. Green, who now understood that I didn't have anywhere to live, was offering me the job of looking after his mother in the daytime. A nurse would stay with her overnight. He would pay me two hundred dollars a week plus room and board. Beyond that, Mrs. Wang explained, Mr. Green would refer patients to me and I could work at his mother's apartment when I had free time. This was a tremendous relief. I realized I could now pay back the thousand dollars my former friend Rose Wong had loaned me to employ Mr. Green's services.

"I'll start today," I said.

I needed only to pick up my two suitcases from Mary, my patient who had given me shelter in my darkest hour. As I walked out of Mr. Green's office, the receptionist Rochelle spoke up.

"When you come back," she said, "I'll take you to my mother's place."

"Your mother?" I was startled and confused. "Rochelle, I'm sorry. I can't work for your mother. I've already promised Mr. Green I'll work for his."

Rochelle smiled. "Mr. Green is my brother."

Mrs. Green's two-bedroom apartment was at the corner of Bathurst Street and Eglinton Avenue. I walked in and saw immediately that it was not only clean but elegantly furnished and hung with good paintings. Rochelle's mother was sitting on her bed.

"Mother, how are you feeling today?" Rochelle asked. Her mother smiled weakly. "I'd like to introduce a wonderful lady. Her name is Hui Zhi Song. She'll live with you and take care of you. Hui Zhi, this is my mother, Ida." Rochelle said to her mother, Ida.

"Hello," said Ida, her voice frail. She looked to be in her early seventies and in a weak condition. Rochelle, with the aid of much hand signalling, showed me my bedroom and the rest of the apartment. Ida was to have much difficulty remembering my first name, so I suggested that she called me "Song." I called her "Grandma," which in the Chinese custom demonstrated respect for an elderly lady.

At about six thirty, Mr. Green came by with dinner. He explained to his mother that I didn't speak English well, but I had a good heart and could be trusted. At eight, the nurse came to do her overnight shift and slept in Grandma's bedroom, which had two beds. The nurse only got up when Grandma needed to use the washroom or if she had an emergency. I found out that Grandma only needed the washroom twice nightly. I felt bad that the Greens had to pay the nurse a

Mendel Green and his Mother Ida
1989

hundred dollars a night for just sleeping there. I offered to do the overnight nursing for Grandma myself to save the nursing care fee for them.

"Are you sure that you don't mind getting up twice a night?" Mr. Green asked.

"Oh, yes." I was confident about this. "It's easy for me."

Mr. Green dismissed the nurse and the next morning was my first day alone with Grandma. I helped her wash her face and clean her teeth. She wanted some cereal for breakfast but I didn't understand what cereal was. She said that it was in a box in the kitchen cupboard. I went to the kitchen and looked around. No box seemed to have "cereal" printed on it. I was confused and embarrassed and after ten minutes I was sweating with anxiety.

"Song, where is my cereal?" Grandma called out.

"Oh, I'm coming! I am coming!" I took a box from the cabinet into her bedroom.

Grandma looked at the box. "That's soda crackers," she said.

I returned to the kitchen and switched the soda crackers for another box. I showed her the box from the doorway.

"No, those are chocolate cookies," she said, she sounded exasperated.

There were only two boxes left in the kitchen. This time I brought both of them, hid one behind my back in my left hand and held out the other, which said "Shredded Wheat."

"Yes! Finally!" she said. Grandma had lost patience with me. How could she know I'd grown up with conge for breakfast for thirty-four years and had never once tasted cereal.

The next morning Grandma was sick and dizzy.

"Give me my Gravol," she demanded, "and a glass of water!"

I couldn't find the Gravol. Her condition rapidly deteriorated. She started vomiting "Gravol," she moaned. "Where's my Gravol?"

I felt terribly guilty and rushed to clean up the mess on the floor. I tried to rub her shoulders to make her feel better. As soon as my hand touched her body, she cried out, "Gravol! Gravol!" I couldn't handle this situation alone and called Rochelle. After half an hour, she came by, but she couldn't find any Gravol either and had to go out to buy some.

After those two incidents, I realized that, even though I cared for Grandma, my English was too poor for me to understand her needs. I told Rochelle that I wasn't the right person to look after her mother and that I wanted to leave.

On the third day, Mr. Green and Rochelle had a meeting in their mother's apartment and agreed that I could leave, but they asked me to stay for two more weeks until they were able to find a suitable replacement. Those two weeks were to change my life.

Only a few days of the two weeks had passed when I realized I had understood Grandma's routine and how to make her feel comfortable. I began to allow myself to relax and one afternoon, while I was washing dishes in the kitchen, I started singing to myself. I walked into Grandma's bedroom and she said smiled.

"Song, you have a beautiful voice. I love to hear you singing. Can you sing for me?"

I sang a happy Chinese song for her. It describes a spring, when the flowers are starting to bloom, the birds are singing and flying, water is flowing in the streams, and children are playing in the garden, the earth is awakening, and everything is alive.

When I was done, she smiled again.

"Can you please sing some more?" she asked.

I thought for a few minutes. "Grandma," I said. I sat on the chair beside her. " I have a lot of sad feelings inside me. If you don't mind, I'll sing a sad song. It's from a Chinese film called "A Little Street" that describes events during the Cultural Revolution. It tells of a girl whose father is a professor and whose mother is a music teacher. They're accused of having Capitalist potential and being American spies. The father is tortured to death and the mother dies of cancer. When the poor child misses her parents, she always sings this song."

I then sang:

When I was a child,
my mother taught a song to me.
without worry or sadness.
Each time I think of it,
it brings me love and warmth.

When I'd finished the song, tears were running down my cheeks.

Grandma held out her arms. "Don't feel sad, Song. Come here, let me hug you,"

She asked me what had made me want to come to Canada and I with my poor English told her about my father's death and my divorce. I didn't tell her about how my mother had treated me because at that time I was still ashamed of it. I told her I'd come to Canada to look for a better life, and especially that I dreamed of being treated as a dignified human being, equally, fairly and respectfully. I told her how lonely I felt and how sometimes I wanted to die so I could see my father again and join the beautiful life in heaven.

"Song!" Grandma looked intensely at me. "Song, I love you! This is your home and your family. You must stay here!"

I was a little shocked and deeply touched and now couldn't hold back and began to cry like a baby. Almost a quarter century after that day in Grandma's room, the voice of that person who was now my new Grandma still rings in my ears—the most powerful words in the world.

From that day on, I felt that someone loved me and cared for me, and needed my love and care in return. Life became meaningful again.

Within a week, Grandma fell ill once more. She suffered from dreadful constipation and although she tried everything, nothing helped. I suffered too, witnessing her suffering, and was able to release some feces using my fingers but even this provided only temporary relief. By Saturday of that week, she was neither eating nor sleeping. Rochelle was out of town for a short vacation and I didn't know what to do. I sat on the bed beside Grandma and put my arm around her shoulder, talking to her to let her know that I was with her. She did not respond but sat motionless, pale and listless. Her arms crossed, staring down at the blanket, trying to handle her nausea. I could see that she might collapse at any time.

The next day I tried to call Rochelle several times but couldn't locate her. I waited anxiously for her to return home. In the afternoon, Grandma finally fell asleep for a while. It made me feel a bit better, and I thought that I would hang on with her until the next day.

On Monday morning, I called Mr. Green's office and told the Chinese secretary that Grandma was very ill and needed to go to hospital immediately. Mr. Green came on the phone and spoke directly to his mother. He asked if he could take her to the hospital but she gave an emphatic "No!"

I kept calling Mr. Green and he said he'd come over. At around eleven in the morning, a nurse came to take some blood samples as a routine follow-up after Grandma's earlier release from the hospital. I complained to the nurse that she needed more blood, not less but she seemed not to understand me. She took three vials of blood and left.

At twelve fifteen, Mr. Green arrived.

"Hi, Mother," he said cheerily. He came close to the bed. "How are you feeling?" he asked. "Can I take to you to the hospital?"

Grandma opened her eyes. "No, no hospital!" she said. At that exact moment her bowel finally moved and a lot of blood made a big mess on her bed. Mr. Green no longer needed his mother's permission. He called an ambulance. When two paramedics arrived, she refused to go and held tightly to her bedpost so that a paramedic had to forcibly release her grip to get her onto the gurney. They took her to the Toronto General Hospital.

At the hospital, a doctor told Mr. Green, Rochelle and I that Grandma had severe stomach bleeding and was in a dangerous coma. Mr. Green and I insisted on staying at the hospital overnight. We slept in chairs and the next morning, I saw Mr. Green buy a newspaper from a paperboy in the waiting area and give the boy five dollars. "Keep the change," he said. When he turned back to me, he saw my questioning eye. "I admire this boy's hard work," he said. "He's selling newspapers before school. He'll be very successful when he grows up, maybe even become famous. You never know."

I didn't respond but I saw further evidence of the kindness of this man and my respect for him grew.

Eventually a doctor came out and talked to Mr. Green for a while. Grandma had survived. Mr Green insisted that I go home for a rest. Grandma stayed in the hospital for two more weeks. During that time, the whole family visited her every day, and I stayed with her full time. Every morning, I washed her face and put some makeup on her. When she wanted to move, I told her to put her arms around my neck, and I moved her slowly and carefully. I sang to her every day. After a week, when she was a bit stronger, I put her in a wheelchair and took her outside to breathe some fresh air and look around the hospital's flower garden, which was surrounded by trees. She seemed comforted by my care and said she believed I was an angel sent to her from God. I was so pleased that I could make her happy.

After two weeks, Grandma was released from the hospital and returned home. Mr. Green had already hired an English lady named Pam to look after her, and I was supposed to leave, according to the original plan. However, I didn't leave, because I now felt this was my home and family, as Grandma had said to me. I moved into Grandma's bedroom and gave up my bedroom to Pam.

During the daytime, it was Pam's job to do all of the housework and take care of Grandma's personal needs, and my job was to look after her during the night. I refused take any pay from Mr. Green, because I strongly believed that family members should take care of each other from the heart, not for money. It was therefore necessary for me to work at my profession. Most days, I went out to do house calls for my old patients and some new ones referred by Mr. Green. I started calling Mr. Green by his first name, Mendel, as I thought a family member should.

It turned out that Pam was not a hard worker. Since she sensed that Grandma trusted me fully, and I could make her more comfortable, she gradually let me take over all of Grandma's personal care. Pam cleaned and cooked and stayed in her bedroom to read books and listen to music during the daytime. I didn't mind doing all of the work to make Grandma feel comfortable, but it was hard for me to build a good relationship with Pam, since she neither worked hard nor showed much compassion.

Grandma liked to sleep with the light on, but this caused me problems. I decided to sleep on the floor so that the shadow of my bed would cut off some of the light and help me get some sleep. She asked me why "Oh, Grandma," I told her. "I just like sleeping on a hard floor because I'm Chinese." Eventually Rochelle discovered the truth and told her mother and that night, Grandma called out, "Song, can you turn off the light for me?"

I was surprised, because I knew she'd be uncomfortable in the dark. "Yes, Grandma," I said. "But why?"

"Just turn it off, dear," she said. It stayed off from that night on.

After we had been living together and caring for each other as loving family members for some months more, Grandma fell sick again and had to go back to the hospital. Mendel put his mother in a private room. "Mendel," she argued. "I don't want to stay here in this private room. It'll cost you too much."

"Don't worry, Mother." Mendel said. "It didn't cost me anything extra." In fact, it had cost him more and I was touched by the deep love between this mother and son.

Pam stayed in the hospital with Grandma during the daytime, and Mendel, Rochelle, and I visited her every day. When I visited her, I always did her makeup and showed her some exercises she could do in her bed. After a week, Mendel went on a business trip to Hong Kong. Before he left, he visited his mother in the hospital to say goodbye to her, and she started crying. It made him feel bad. He tried to cheer her up and stayed beside her bed as long as possible. Shortly after Mendel left, Grandma went into a coma. The Green family, including the other daughter from Ottawa and all the grandchildren, rotated staying with her during the night. Since Pam didn't work on Sundays, my job was to stay in the hospital with Grandma full time for the day.

On October 26th, 1986, on Sunday morning at four thirty A.M., the phone rang. It was Rochelle. It had been her turn to stay at the hospital overnight with her son. She said, "Hui Zhi, my son has caught a cold, and I'm very tired. We both want to go home. Can you come to the hospital a few hours early?"

"I'll come now," I replied.

"Call the taxi, and I'll pay the fare," she said. She knew that I normally went to the hospital by bus and subway to save a few dollars.

I arrived shortly after five in the morning to switch with the family. Grandma was still in the coma. I used a wet towel to clean her face then started singing to her as I customarily did. At seven, Stephen, Mendel's oldest son, came to visit. He was an immigration lawyer like his father. We sat in Grandma's room and chatted for a while, then Stephen said, "Hui Zhi, let's go for breakfast."

"You go, I'll stay with Grandma," I answered.

About twenty minutes after he left, Grandma called out. "God!" she called. I got up and walked quickly to her bed. She suddenly moved, breathing with difficulty. She opened her mouth wide and twisted her body, clenching her hands tightly to try to breathe more easily. It was as though she was battling with the devil and calling on God for help. Then she stopped breathing with her eyes and mouth still open and I knew that she was gone. It was the first time in my life that I had seen with my own eyes the final moment of life. I saw the effort of her struggle to stay alive. My heart pounded so fast and loud that not only could I hear it, but I also felt that it would jump out of my throat. I pushed the emergency button. A nurse came and put her fingers on Grandma's neck to check her pulse then left to call a doctor to confirm the death.

I picked up the phone and called Rochelle. "Come! Come quickly, please!"

She didn't need to ask why.

While I waited for the doctor and Rochelle to come, I went to Grandma's bed and put my hand on her body. It was still warm. I closed her eyes and mouth, relaxed her fists and straightened her twisted body to make her look peaceful, even though it hadn't been easy for her to give up her life.

"Grandma," I whispered. "You're in God's hands now. Please enjoy your peaceful life in heaven."

Stephen returned to the room. "Grandma is gone," I told him.

Rochelle arrived shortly after a doctor had confirmed Grandma's death. She cried for a while then made many calls to family and relatives, including her brother overseas. She then began to make the funeral arrangements.

We waited for Mendel to rush back from Hong Kong. The funeral was held in London, Ontario, and Grandma was buried beside her husband in a city where they had once lived. God had taken the only family I had, the only person who loved me and needed my love in return.

I stayed in Grandma's apartment alone for two more months, then found a two-bedroom apartment to share with three Chinese students downtown. I slept alone in a tiny bedroom, the other two girls shared a large bedroom, and a young man slept in the living room. Our apartment had only one small bathroom. It was crowded in the morning, so I took my shower at night before I went to sleep.

I picked up a single mattress on the street and bought a small desk, a plastic chair and a telephone from a garage sale. With Rochelle's permission I took some dishes, towels and bedding from Grandma's old home. All of my clothing was second hand and came from donations. I didn't own a pair of winter boots that fit, so I put some cotton inside the ones I had. I managed to spend only two hundred dollars a month, which included a hundred and thirty for the room, thirty-seven for a transit pass and thirty-three dollars for food. I survived on milk, bread and bananas.

June, 1986

I started doing house calls for acupuncture and massage, going by subway and bus. I'd met an old Chinese lady who'd been sick in the Toronto General Hospital at the same time as Grandma. The day Grandma passed away, she'd seen how deeply I was affected and told me how she wished her own daughter would show such sorrow when she died. Her husband was disabled, needed a wheelchair, and lived in a subsidized retirement home and when she realized I had no familial relationship with Grandma, she asked me to look after her as well. She couldn't afford to hire me full-time but she asked me to come on Sundays to prepare food for the week and cook Sunday's lunch. She only paid me ten dollars for three hours of work and I travelled for an hour to get there. I took the job to make her feel better and for the extra forty dollars a month.

I was to live for many years in this way, keeping alive my dream of a better future.

11

In Search of Home

July, 1989

In the summer of 1989, Mendel set up a Canadian immigration interview in Los Angeles for me. Stephen, his lawyer son, offered to accompany me. As before, I had to leave Canada and apply for landed immigrant status from outside the country. Stephen was planning to go to Los Angeles for a Taiwanese client's immigration interview, and he asked his father to reschedule my interview to match his client's.

When we arrived at Pearson airport, I started to limp because my tight shoes chaffed the skin of my heels. The shoes were almost new, a gift from a kind friend, but they were too small. Stephen put bandages on my heels and said, "Let me be your father and take care of you," he said.

"No," I protested. "You're not my father. You're younger than me." I pretended to argue with him but I was warmed by his words. When we arrived in Los Angeles, he stayed in a fancy downtown hotel paid for by his client. I stayed at the home of one of my former patients who had received many acupuncture treatments from me when she was visiting Toronto.

My interview was on Friday, July 15th. On Thursday, Stephen successfully concluded his client's interview and was invited to a dinner in a very nice Chinese restaurant to celebrate with his client with some friends. He took me with him as an "interpreter." I was nervous about this role. Fortunately, the Taiwanese client's English was much worse than mine, and no one noticed whether I was interpreting incorrectly. After dinner, Stephen advised me to stay in his room, because his hotel was close to the immigration office.

The next morning at five, Stephen left to catch his flight to Toronto. I'd tossed and turned all night, I was so worried about my interview. After Steven left for the airport, I got up to practice my limited English.

My interview was at nine. I waited anxiously in the waiting area. At nine fifteen, my name was called. The immigration officer was a middle-aged woman and after a few minutes, I felt comfortable with her friendly, patient demeanour. I soon began to feel more confident. She asked me to explain each course I'd studied in Chinese medicine school, and I tried my best to describe them to her, until I came to the anatomy course. I didn't know how to explain properly in English, and fumbling for the words.

"The anatomy is about opening the dead body's chest to learn all of human organs, including the bones and nerve systems," I told her. She didn't laugh at me but kept smiling and showed great interest in what I was saying.

After about half an hour, she put down her pen. "Congratulations," she said. "You've passed your independent landed immigration interview. When you return to Canada, you'll become a Canadian landed immigrant as soon as an immigration officer puts a stamp on your papers." She stood up and shook my hand.

I rushed back to the hotel and closed the door "Oh, Hui Zhi!" I cried. "You're officially a Canadian immigrant now! You don't have to bend to anyone who wants to take advantage of you! You don't need to worry about being deported to China! You're equal to any other Canadian immigrant. You can go to school to study English properly and get reasonable pay when you work. Oh, Hui Zhi, your miserable life is over! You will have a bright future. This is the last time you'll cry. Enjoy your happy tears now, because you won't have any cause later for sadness any more!"

I wept. I felt my tears washing my wounds. I grew more and more relaxed, until, tired of crying, I fell asleep in a chair. When I woke, I felt much better. I gave the room key to the front desk and returned to my patient's friend's home for the rest of my stay.

On Saturday, I paid $29.99 for a day trip by bus to Disneyland, since I had missed going there on my first trip to Los Angeles. I'd never had so much fun in my life as I did on that day. It was a special day, a day to celebrate my Canadian immigration. My eyes and my mouth were open wide as saucers at discovering how those amazing Hollywood tricks were done. I was selected from the audience to wear a nineteenth century western costume and asked to stand onstage making motions with my hands. After stepping down, I saw myself on film, riding a speeding horse along with other movie stars, trying to escape pursuing outlaws. I laughed and laughed just like a child. It was a remarkable day.

When I returned to Toronto on Monday after the weekend in Los Angeles, as my cheap ticket required, I was concerned about making the payment for my legal fees. My work permit and independent immigration legal fee totalled seven thousand Canadian dollars. I had already paid half of that total, including a thousand dollars borrowed from Rose Wong. Now I needed to pay Mendel the other half to close up my account and was still three hundred and fifty dollars short. It took me a week to do any and all possible work to gather the remaining money. I was now ready to go to Mendel's office as his client.

On Monday morning I went to the office and spoke to Rochelle.

She announced, "Hui Zhi is here. She got her landed immigrant status!"

The many lawyers and secretaries emerged from their offices, came to the reception area and cheered me. "Congratulations, Hui Zhi!" they called. Some shook hands with me, and some even hugged me. I was surprised and moved. I hadn't known that so many people cared.

"Where were you?" Stephen said. "Why didn't you come here a week ago? I was worried about you!" In the middle of the excitement and celebration, Mendel came out to join us.

He took me into his office, and as soon as the door closed, I took the three thousand five hundred dollars cash from my pocket and said, "Thanks, Mendel. This is the money I owe you."

"Hui Zhi." Mendel shook his head. "Don't you mention anything about money. You don't owe me anything."

"No," I argued. "This is your business. I have to pay you."

"Hui Zhi, you looked after my mother as if she were your own. You saved her life. Forget the money. If you mention it one more time, I will be angry with you!" He hugged me.

I cried on Mendel's shoulder like a baby and left my tears along with black and red make-up on his clean white shirt.

Chapter Eleven

As a landed immigrant, I was allowed to study English as a second language for new immigrants, paid for by the government. I studied from nine A.M. to three P.M. After class, I worked as an acupuncturist and masseuse from five P.M. to seven P.M. at a downtown chiropractic office that I'd found through Mendel's connections. This chiropractic doctor only charged me a hundred dollars a month and allowed me to work in his clinic when he wasn't there. I also did house calls by subway and bus until I returned most days to my home at midnight. I was exhausted by my studies and by work. My pillow became my best friend. I wanted someday to buy a car and a house for myself and continue my education. To reach those goals, I knew that I must make as much money as possible and save as much as possible.

One afternoon, I fell asleep during my English class, and a classmate, Mr. Chou, who came from Hong Kong, asked me, "Miss Song, what are you doing after school? Why are you so tired?"

I told him that after a whole day at school, I had to work until midnight to make money to support myself and to save.

"Oh, I can show you an easy and fast way to make money, if you can find a few free hours," he said.

On Monday of the next week, I scheduled myself to start work at six P.M. and reserved three hours for Mr. Chou. He drove me to Bayview and 16th Avenues in a suburb north of Toronto and stopped in front of a new house.

"Is this your home?" I asked.

He didn't answer, just opened the door and let me in. "It's a beautiful house," I said.

He showed me around the house then took me outside so I could view the surrounding area. "There are twenty new houses nearby that are ready for sale," he said. "Would you like to live in one of them?"

"Me? How could I possibly buy a beautiful house like one of these? I have no money. Maybe I can buy one in five years, if I'm lucky."

"Don't worry, I can help you." He took me to his friend's house.

"This is my friend, Mr. Chen," Mr. Chou said. "He can help you buy a house."

"How much money do you have now?" Mr. Chen asked.

"I have five thousand dollars savings," I answered.

Mr. Chen nodded. "If you give me the five thousand and sign your name on this paper, I'll return twenty thousand to you a year from now. You can use the money to put a down payment on a new house."

This was too good to believe. I pulled Mr. Chou aside. "Is this possible? What's your friend doing?"

"Don't worry, Miss Song," Mr. Chou said. "It's possible. My friend is a magic investor. He can get the money you need."

"But how?" I asked again.

"It's all about using the stock market to invest money, but it's too complicated to explain to you, since you come from mainland China," he said. "Do you think Canada is a good country?"

"Yes," I answered.

"Then just trust that this wonderful country will make your dream come true," said Mr. Chou. "You just put money in the market and let it grow. It's a magical place to grow your money fast."

I recalled other heartening moments, I remembered the day I'd arrived at a Canadian airport and received such wonderful service and such a warm welcome. I remembered the time I'd received my work permit in Los Angeles, when I couldn't read English and the immigration officer told me to just sign my name. All of my good memories came out.

The ways of this wonderful country were beyond my understanding. I signed the paper at the place Mr. Chen showed me. I gave him five thousand dollars in cash the next day.

A month later, I received a letter with a lot of numbers on it that I couldn't interpret. I took it to the English school to show Mr. Chou. He told me that the letter was not important and to just ignore it. The next month, I received a similar letter, along with another letter with IMPORTANT written on the envelope. I couldn't understand what the letter said, but I sensed that I shouldn't ignore it. I had a patient named Peter Martin, the managing director of a major investment banking firm. I didn't understand what the firm did, but I knew that Mr. Martin had an important position. He carried a heavy briefcase full of financial papers to his downtown office every day. The heavy briefcase had caused him to develop shoulder pain, and I'd given him a number of acupuncture and shiatsu treatments at the chiropractic clinic. I'd also advised him to leave the heavy briefcase at the office, but he said he had to read all those papers at home.

When Mr. Martin came to the clinic, near the end of the treatment, while he was still lying face down on the table, I asked if he would read the letter for me. I gave him the letter marked IMPORTANT. He read it quickly. "Oh, my god!" he exclaimed. "What did you buy to lose that much money?"

"I don't know," I said, confused.

"Where are all the statements you received?"

"What is a statement?" I asked.

"Have you received other mailings with a lot of numbers

on them?"

"Oh, yes, I have two," I answered.

"Where are those statements?"

"At my apartment."

"Can you bring those letters to my office tomorrow?" he said urgently. "It's very important. There's a big problem here." He drew up a map showing me how to get to his office.

When I went there, he read the statements carefully then asked me to explain how I'd become involved in the financial market with such a speculative investment firm. I told him what had happened in my poor English. He wrote the number $12,000 on a piece of paper and told me, "Your investment advisor bought silver futures on margin for you. You lost $12,000 in two months, and they are saying you have to put more money in. Do you have any more money?"

I was shocked. I didn't know how to react, so I just said, "No, I have no money, but they promised to give me twenty thousand a year later."

He gazed at me for a few seconds, then he said, "You leave all these papers with me, and I will try my best to help you." He told me this was a clear-cut case of inappropriate investing by my broker, and he was willing to take my situation to a regulatory authority, in this case the Toronto Stock Exchange, which everyone called the TSE.

He called the Exchange to report my story and set up a meeting with exchange officials to review my situation. After a week, he took me to the Exchange office with all my paperwork, and before the meeting started, he instructed me to tell them my story.

"But my English is not good enough to describe the whole thing," I said, worried.

"Don't worry, just tell them what you told me. Your English

is good enough to make people understand," he said. He also said that he would point out anything I might miss.

Peter tried to boost my confidence. "Fundamental bank brokerage rules and regulations have been broken here," he explained. "There are rules regarding knowing your client and knowing the investments that are suitable for them. That's something the exchange officials will want to jump on, because situations like this make honest brokers look bad."

The meeting started at two, with three TSE officials present, as well as Peter and me. We sat around a long meeting table, and I told them the story of how I'd become involved in the stock market.

I finished and Peter turned to the others.

"Miss Song came to our country from Communist China with only sixty dollars to build a better life," he said, and there was strong feeling in his voice. "She knew almost no English when she came here, but she studies our language and works extremely hard. The broker she met knew that Miss Song didn't have any experience with the stock market. He invested her money in the riskiest of high-risk investments on margin. Miss Song's money should have been in safe securities. She lost four year's savings, plus twelve thousand more! I'm shocked to see someone treated so badly by her broker. I think it's a criminal act, and I ask strongly that you investigate this case and help Miss Song get her money back."

The TSE officials seemed nervous at this aggressive approach, because the brokerage company involved was a member firm of the TSE. One lady asked Peter what he wanted the TSE to do.

Peter sat back for a minute. "Well, personally,"—his tone was thoughtful—"Personally, I'd raid the office and shut the broker down."

They all looked terribly uneasy.

"I'm a senior partner of a major investment firm," Peter continued. "You know quite well our firm is far more important to the TSE than this other outfit. If you don't go in and get this broker, I'll take this to the newspapers and let them tell this woman's story. We in this business must deal with the bad apples, because one makes all of us and our businesses look bad."

Suddenly I wasn't frightened. This man couldn't speak a word of Chinese, but in great contrast to Mr. Chen, he was willing to protect me forcefully. His qualities showed me again that humanity, compassion, and decency do matter and are far more important than money and material things.

The meeting lasted about an hour, and the TSE officials agreed to further investigate the case. They gave me their business cards and told me to go home and wait. The suspense was awful.

The phone rang one morning a week later. Was it Peter? No, it was the wife of the broker Mr. Chen. She was extremely angry and swore at me in guttural Cantonese. Apparently the TSE had raided the brokerage office and opened an investigation on Mr. Chen. Shortly afterwards, I received a death threat call from an unknown male voice. Frightened, I reported the call to the TSE right away.

Although I had signed my name and agreed to let Mr. Chen become my stockbroker, I hadn't by chance authorized Mr. Chen to act independently on the stock market on my behalf. He had tried to get me to sign that form after my loss, which may have given him that authority, but Peter told me not to. Peter had determined that Mr. Chen had bought and sold silver futures contracts on margin several times without my knowledge and agreement, so the TSE decided that Mr.

Chen and I each owed half of the twelve thousand dollars lost from my account. Since I didn't have any money, they gave me a generous length of time to pay back the six thousand dollars. The TSE warned Mr. Chen that if they received one more complaint, he would lose his license. They also warned him that if anyone ever hurt me, he would be the prime suspect.

I now realized that Canada might be a free country, but that did not mean that materials or services came free. I would have to work hard to get the things I wanted. I also learned that I had to read a document carefully before signing. As soon as I signed, I was responsible. Every country has both good and bad people, and it was my job to protect myself.

Mendel and Peter referred more patients to me. Before Christmas, Peter bought ten massage gift certificates from me for his staff's Christmas presents. I was very fortunate to have those two extremely kind and caring people in my life. Also, I was lucky to have built up a reputation as having "magic hands" and demand for my traditional Chinese medical service was growing. Many people treated me as their emergency doctor, realizing that day or night, workday or holiday, I was always there for them. I paid back the six thousand dollars and not long after bought the first car in my life, a tiny Nissan.

Since I'd left home in 1985, my mother had continued in her desire that her son live with her in Shanghai. According to the government's policy on family relocation, he could return home if Mother didn't have another one of her children living with her, provided that his company would agree to release him. By leaving home for Canada, I had left my space open for my brother to return, but his company had refused to grant him permission.

Now my mother asked me to talk to my brother's boss in person. She wanted me to meet the boss at my brother's hometown in Maansan, a small city close to Nanjing. At that time, China treated overseas Chinese as honourable guests because the government needed to promote a favourable reputation in the West, so Mother reasoned that my appeal to my brother's boss might help. After four and half years of a difficult life in Canada, I was also homesick. The airfare would cost me over a thousand dollars but I agreed. In the spring of 1990, I flew home.

I picked up my luggage, walked out and breathed the air of my hometown for the first time in five years. Outside the baggage area of Shanghai airport crowds of people waited to meet their families and friends from overseas. I looked at those excited or anxious strangers' faces, and was filled with loneliness and sadness hit me. Five years earlier I'd left my home alone with my tears, and no one had been with me at that same airport to bid me farewell. After years of struggling, here I was alone again in China with fresh tears and no one to welcome me.

I checked into a modest hotel and went after dinner to see the house in which I'd been born. There was no one home and I didn't have a key, so I walked around the area a few times. When I returned to the hotel, it was late, so I closed the door, lay on the bed and wept. After some time a hotel staff member came into the room without knocking.

"Are you alright, little comrade?" I looked up. It was a middle-aged man. I jumped up from the bed.

"Who are you?" I demanded. "How did you get into my room?"

"Don't misunderstand me," he said softly. "I work here. I'm checking on you because I heard you crying for so long that I wanted to help you."

"I'm fine, thank you," I said. He left. I looked at my watch. It was two thirty in the morning. I told myself that tomorrow would be a better day and the sun would shine on me again.

I bought a train ticket to my brother's town, about a seven-hour ride from Shanghai. There wasn't anyone waiting for me at that destination either. I took a bus and walked for about an hour, trying to find his home based on the confusing instructions my mother had mailed to me. I found it at last—and my mother and brother and my brother's family. The next day, he took me to his company's office for a meeting with his manager, where I simply repeated the words that my brother had written for me. The manager agreed to transfer my brother to Shanghai soon.

So I completed my mission as Mother had requested and a few months later, my brother was back in Shanghai and living at home on the third floor in my old room. I received no word of appreciation from either of them.

12 Still Searching

November, 1992

As soon as I had my work permit, I was determined to repay Rose Wong the thousand dollars she'd lent me. I called her and we agreed to meet at her new house in Forest Hill, one of the most expensive areas in Toronto. I drove there one afternoon in the summer of 1986.

Her French-style furniture and nineteenth-century oil paintings made me feel like I was standing in an art gallery. We sat in the kitchen, which was bigger than my living room, and I put a cheque for one thousand dollars on the kitchen table.

"Rose, I'd like to pay back the money that you loaned me," I said. I pushed the cheque over to her.

"No." She shook her head. "You just got your work permit and you don't have much money. I can wait until you get your citizenship."

She pushed the cheque back over to my side of the table. After we had slid the thousand dollars back and forth a few times, I relented and put it in my pocket.

Chapter Twelve

> Neither a borrower nor a lender be,
> For loan oft loses both itself and friend,
> And borrowing dulls the edge of husbandry.

I'd always understood Shakespeare's Polonius to mean that when we lend money to another, we make a friend, but when we want our money back, we make an enemy. But I'd decided that Polonius was wrong. When Rose had lent the money to me, it had been in a spirit of generosity and kindness, and when I tried to pay back the money, she saw my honesty. Through that thousand-dollar loan we were able to recognize the good qualities in each other once more, and our friendship was resumed. When I started socializing frequently with Rose and her family, I discovered that her husband loved his wife and children deeply and was generous to his friends. When I was granted landed immigrant status in 1989, I tried once more to repay Rose. She told me that she'd never intended to ask me to pay her back, but I insisted. Finally she accepted.

In the autumn of 1990, I officially became a Canadian citizen. As I raised my arm to swear the oath and sang the words of the Canadian national anthem, I felt my blood flowing hot and fast, and my tears—which had flowed so often in sadness—flowed once more. O Canada, our home and native land.

The day after I became a citizen, Rose, in a gesture of incredible generosity, treated me to a trip to Paris. She said it was important that the first stamp on my Canadian passport should be from my dream country. We visited the Louvre and saw all of the famous paintings and sculptures including the famous Mona Lisa. In the evening we walked along the banks of the Seine and sang and danced at the Louvre's new glass Piermont Square. Later we visited the opera house and took in a stage show at the Lido. As I walked through the street holding a rose, a gift from a restaurant owner, Rose saw a beautiful antique car driving by. She stopped the car in the middle of the street and told me to stand in front of it so she could take a picture of me. I realized that we had stopped the traffic, but no one was angry. The other drivers were smiling or saying "Ooh-la-la!" It was though I was a bird in flight after the cage door has been opened.

I returned to my real life. At that time, acceptance of acupuncture wasn't as prevalent as it is today—most of my working hours were spent giving massage therapy. Massage is a physically demanding job and I was not eating properly. I began to develop my own sore neck, back, and fingers. Sometimes, after I had bent over for too long, when I stood upright, I felt dizzy and lost my vision for a few seconds. Besides the physical difficulty, my work schedule only allowed time to work in the chiropractic clinic after five on weekdays and full days on weekends. I was doing a house call almost every night to make ends meet. I would find myself caught in frightening thunderstorms at midnight and of course I worried about these lonely visits to strangers. On night I broke a rib negotiating a slippery staircase in the dark and lay at home in pain for two weeks without going to a doctor or hospital. No one visited me. I ate soda crackers and drank water to survive and passed the time reading books. Loneliness haunted me again. It was time to get more education and change my career, I decided. I was now almost forty.

Canada did not accept my Chinese educational qualifications. No one would hire me as a mechanical engineer or allow me to practice as an acupuncture doctor in a hospital or clinic. I would have to start over again at a Canadian university and to gain entrance, I would need to pass the TOEFL English test for foreign students. I also had to save enough money to pay the tuition fees and support myself during my studies. In 1991, after I'd tried three times to pass the TOEFL test, I got the minimum score necessary to allow me to continue my university studies. First I went to a chiropractic school in Toronto to ask if it would accept me as a student but exempt me from the first two years of study. I showed them my acupuncture diploma, which proved that I had already studied anatomy and basic Western medical concepts, and knew how to read blood tests and X-rays. They would not agree. It was disappointing, but I would not give up.

Terry was a patient of mine and a professor at McMaster University. She told me one day that McMaster, which is in Hamilton, Ontario, had started a two year full-time physiotherapy course. It required a bachelor's degree from any country and a minimum average of eighty percent. This was wonderful news, since I fit that requirement. To make my case for acceptance even stronger, I started working as a volunteer once a week in the Mount Sinai Hospital physiotherapy department, the best hospital for that treatment in Toronto.

In the spring of 1992, and with Terry's help, I finished the thirty pages of a long application form. Then with my bachelor's degree documents translated, my TOEFL test scores, ten month's volunteer work at Mount Sinai Hospital and an evaluation letter, I applied for entry. Terry volunteered to deliver my application, since she worked there. I was confident I'd be accepted but nonetheless waited anxiously for two months before finally receiving the letter from McMaster. The answer was no. The letter didn't even provide a reason.

I had no energy or interest in anything for two months. I simply stayed at home, sleeping and wondering why I could not find acceptance after working so hard. Terry went to the McMaster physiotherapy department to ask for an explanation. The answer came as a surprise. "Ms Song isn't an independent person," she was told. "She didn't even send in the application herself."

The committee hadn't even read my application. Canada was in a recession and apparently too many people wanted to return to school. The university only had room for one percent of all the students who had applied. It could afford to be choosy.

I decided to drive to McMaster myself, determined to speak face to face with someone in the department. I went up to the physiotherapy department, my heart pounding, and gave my name to the receptionist. I explained that I had to speak to the person who was in charge of registration. Then I sat down in the otherwise empty reception area and waited. At length the receptionist looked up.

"Sarah Burr will see you now. She's the assistant registrar."

She gestured towards a doorway and I followed the corridor to a door with "Sarah Burr, Assistant Registrar" printed on a plaque. I knocked.

"Come in?" a voice responded as though asking a question.

A prim woman of perhaps forty sat behind a surprisingly small desk. She gestured to a chair.

"I'm Sarah Barr," she informed me without warmth. "I'm assistant registrar. What can I do for you?"

"My name is Hui Zhi Song," I said. "I applied to study your physiotherapy program. I want to know why I was rejected."

I handed her the letter I'd received from the department. She looked it over quickly. "This clearly explains why we can't accept you," she said. "What else do you want?" She handed the letter back to me.

"It didn't explain why I wasn't accepted," I said. "Can you

look at it again?"

"No, Miss Song, I can't give you any more answers. In fact, I'm afraid I'm quite busy."

She looked down at her paperwork, pointedly ignoring me. I stood silent and uncomfortable. Finally I spoke.

"I heard I wasn't accepted to study because I didn't hand in the application myself and that was why someone in your department decided I'm not an independent person. That person didn't even look at my application."

Sarah Burr raised her head and looked at me. After a long moment, she sniffed and almost seemed to shrug.

"Ms. Song, perhaps, if you didn't hand in the application yourself as you've just said, you are not an independent person."

I stared at her, dumbfounded. She was talking about my life, not my application—my entire life.

"What kind of person is independent from your point of view?" I asked, feeling anger rise inside me. "I arrived here with sixty dollars and a three-month visitor's visa, with no family in Canada, and no English. Is that not independent? I passed my English test after just two and half years of study. The whole time I worked extremely hard to support myself. I saved money to study at university. Do I deserve to be judged as lacking independence? Do I?" I thrust my head forward a little and Sarah Burr drew back a little. "You know what? You know what? Life is too easy for you! You, you don't know the meaning of independent!"

I fled then but within hours discovered that my outburst had cured my depression. A rejection by McMaster University was not the end. It occurred to me that I'd been crying much of my life. Now I stopped crying. How could I best use of the money I'd so painfully saved for my education?

Postscript

1993-2009

From 1992 to 1999 Song Hui Zhi lived in the house she'd bought on Summerhill Gardens while she worked as a therapist at a nearby headache- and pain-management clinic. She played cello with the Etobicoke Symphony for twelve years and the Mississauga Symphony for three years, touring in Vienna, Paris, and Prague.

Hui Zhi Song among the string section of the Mississauga Orchestra

A Trinket Seller in XinJiang
oil on canvas
Song Hui Zhi

In May of 1999, she graduated from the Ontario College of Art and Design, majoring in oil painting. She taught art to children for some time but has continued her own painting: still lifes, landscapes and portraits of those, young and old, she has met on her travels in recent years.

In June 1999, Song Hui Zhi married Bill Mitchell, a nuclear engineer, and from May, 2001 to September, 2003, she lived in China and was engaged in charity work while her husband was part of the team overseeing the construction of a nuclear power station that employed Canadian CANDU technology. She organized the 2002 Canadian Thanksgiving Charity Dinner for expatriate Canadians in China, attended by a hundred and fifty people, with the proceeds going to local Chinese children for medication and education. She met Canadian Prime Minister Jean Chrétien during his trip that year to China. She visited her family and posed for a group photograph in 2002.

A visit to Shanghai in 2002
BACK: My brother Wei De's wife, Wei De, me, Bill, Hui Li, Hui Min.
FRONT: Wei De's son, Hui Ping, Mother, Hui Ling, Hui Guo.

Song Hui Zhi visited her mother and sent her money frequently, which improved their relationship but caused her brother to worry that his mother would leave the house to Hui Zhi and not to himself. When she discovered this, Hui Zhi requested that her mother leave the family house equally to all seven of her children in equal shares. In 2003, when her mother underwent a gall bladder operation, Hui Zhi paid to put her in a private hospital room.

Oct. 23, 2001. Rt. Hon. Jean Chretien with Hui Zhi Song during Chretien's visit as Prime Minister to the Canadian expat staff at Quinshan Nuclear Power project

In 2004, Hui Zhi wrote her mother a letter describing the pain of her childhood. She argued that her twenty years of independent living in Canada and the fact that she had sent money routinely was proof that she had never wanted to take anything from her mother. Thereafter, mother and daughter were again somewhat estranged.

In 2004, Hui Zhi learned to play duplicate bridge, and was named Rookie of the Year for Southern Ontario. Three years later, she earned a Life Master Certificate in the American Contract Bridge League. In 2006, she was baptized a Christian and that same year graduated from the Transformational Arts College as a spiritual psychotherapist. In May of 2009, she became a foster parent to a Ugandan girl named Miriam.

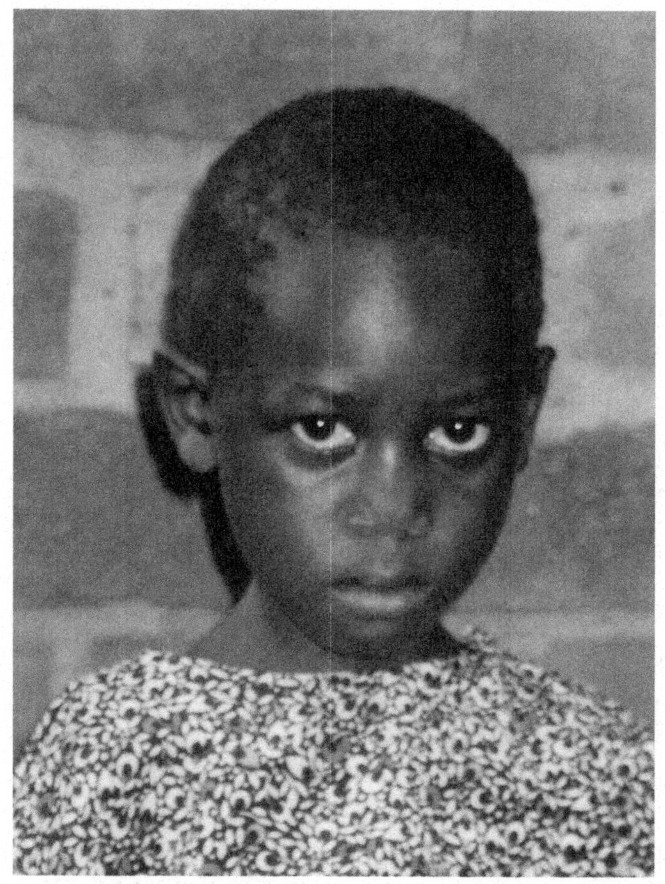

Song's Ugandan Foster Child, Mariam

In March of that same year, her mother passed away in Shanghai at the age of ninety, leaving her share of the family home to her only son.

In Appreciation

I began writing this book on several occasions but the painful memories it evoked prevented me from continuing. I felt tremendous shame at being treated so badly by my birth mother and I feared telling the truth about my miserable life in China while I was under Chairman Mao's and my mother's control. I often struggled to forget the whole thing but when I finally got down to it, I was able to keep going—and find peace and love—only with the help of many others.

I want to express my gratitude to all my teachers at the Transformational Arts College in Toronto, to Dr. Peter Bernstein and to May Jackson, a friend who had also suffered from the treatment she received from her mother and who healed herself beautifully. Through telling me her personal story and through her gentle approach, she helped me move forward more easily.

I have already described my enormous debt of gratitude to the Green family and more words could not increase that gratitude.

Although I have lived in Canada for twenty-five years, I studied English as a new immigrant for only two and half